The Praeter-Colonial Mind

An Intellectual Journey Through the Back Alleys of
Empire

FRANCISCO LOBO

E-INTERNATIONAL
RELATIONS
PUBLISHING

E-International Relations
Bristol, England
2025

ISBN: 978-1-910814-72-7

Production: Michael Tang
Cover Image: frankie_s (Francesco Chiesa)/Depositphotos.

A catalogue record for this book is available from the British Library.

E-International Relations

Editor-in-Chief and Publisher: Stephen McGlinchey
Editorial assistance: Ibrahim Atta, Anton Bronfman, Evan Smith.

E-International Relations is the world's leading International Relations website and publisher. Our daily publications feature expert articles, reviews, podcasts and interviews – as well as student learning resources. The website is run by a non-profit organisation based in Bristol, England and staffed by an all-volunteer team. In addition to our website content, E-International Relations publishes a range of books.

As E-International Relations is committed to open access in the fullest sense, free versions of our books are available on our website https://www.e-ir.info/

Abstract

The Praeter-Colonial Mind: An Intellectual Journey Through the Back Alleys of Empire attempts to understand the many ways in which, for good or ill, the lingering legacies of imperialism play a key role in our post-colonial societies of today. Drawing on anecdotal evidence and philosophical analysis, its contents span across the war in Ukraine, British and American imperialism, the so-called Global South, anti-colonialism and decolonization, culture wars and political violence, Trumpism, the rules-based international order, the rise of China, and the advent of AI, all against the backdrop of the author's personal experiences in America, Europe, and post-Soviet spaces. The mind that tries to make sense of all of this is the praeter-colonial mind, a mind that, in accordance with the varied meanings of the prefix 'praeter' (namely 'past, by, beyond, above, more than, in addition to, besides') sees colonialism simultaneously as past and present as it is confronted with the evidence of its many legacies. A mind that, in the end, attempts to step aside to gain perspective and go above and beyond colonialism for the sake of the present and the future.

About the author

Francisco Lobo holds a PhD in War Studies from King's College London. He also holds an LLM in International Legal Studies (New York University), an LLM in International Law and an LLB (University of Chile). He has worked as a legal practitioner in the private and public sectors. He has more recently worked as an advisor for an international development project to train the Armed Forces of Ukraine in IHL and military ethics standards. His research focuses on international law, human rights, the laws and ethics of war, legal theory, moral philosophy, and history.

For Kimberly, my sunshine, love of my life,

who always finds a place for me in her dreams,

who believes in me beyond comprehension,

and who encouraged me to write this book

the second the title left my lips.

Contents

Introduction

Tough Times

What is happening to the world? The late José 'Pepe' Zalaquett, a renowned human rights lawyer who stood up for justice and truth against the atrocities committed by Pinochet in Chile and beyond, used to say that what we are experiencing after the Cold War may very well not be a 'time of change' ('época de cambios'), but a true 'epochal change' ('cambio de época'). It is for future historians to decide whether or not he was right. Yet, his words carry significant weight for the reader of the present, as there is no denying that with the advent of Donald Trump's second presidency we are observing a 'direction of travel' that for many points to the end of the rules-based order established after World War II (Cordall 2025).

Whether times of change or the days of an epochal change, ours can surely be called '*tiempos recios*', or 'tough times'. These are the words that Santa Teresa de Ávila, a Spanish nun, chose to characterize her own times, the sixteenth century in Europe, rife with religious wars, invasions, disease and controversies surrounding imperial expansion and matters of conscience. They seem also quite suitable to describe our tumultuous twenty-first century so far.

How is it possible to gain any understanding of our times? Hannah Arendt once described the epistemological attitude of the ancients as 'wonder', until the Age of Reason, and Descartes in particular, turned that sense of wonder into the methodic 'doubt', or doubt as a way of seeing the world in front of us (Arendt 1998, 275). In our age of post-truth and pervasive online vitriol, it is hard to say what our epistemological attitude is. It is certainly not an attitude of doubt – otherwise, most misinformation and conspiracy theories would be met with an impenetrable wall of logic and we would all be better for it. But it is also not an attitude of simple wonder, as the world does not seem to surprise us anymore – so much so that, not content with believing we know everything about the past and the present, some even call themselves 'futurists', namely professionals who predict trends and developments in all things technological and political.

The epistemological attitude of our day, rather, seems to be a unique blend of a sort of 'caustic doubt' that challenges all canons, understandings, and institutions for the sole sake of dismantling them; and a 'supine wonder' that renders us completely defenseless in the face of overwhelming amounts of data and the information technologies delivering it to our doorstep, or to our fingertips. The epistemic attitude that is the praeter-colonial mind presented in this work is one step in the right direction to move us away from these perils. But we should all be mindful that no one book will hold all the answers to the questions that afflict us today.

I am, naturally, not exempt from these flawed outlooks. However, I like to think that going outside of my comfort zone has helped me to overcome them at least in part. As fate would have it, my wife's work led us to a place where some of the most important issues of the day, including war, misinformation, decolonization and the fight for self-determination, are in full display and unfolding at a vertiginous speed: Ukraine. After many years of studying war and political violence through the pristine lens of law and ethics, I was finally afforded the opportunity to see a society at war from up close. Ironically, around the same time I was working on a chapter about a sixteenth century Spanish priest, Alonso de la Vera Cruz, a contemporary of Santa Teresa de Ávila and protagonist of her fabled tough times who defended the rights of indigenous peoples in colonial Mexico, not contenting himself with staying behind and pontificating about the New World from the Old one. 'I speak from experience' he would famously remark (Lobo 2025, 59). It could be said that I had my own 'Vera Cruz moment' when I was lucky enough to go see Ukraine. This reflection and all of the ones that follow and that make up this book are the result of such an experience.

But unlike Vera Cruz, I am not confronted with the main issues of imperialism in its early stages. What I saw in Ukraine belongs in the opposite end of the long arc of colonial history: a process of decolonization and the search for self-determination that has resulted in a valiant and bloody war of self-defense against foreign aggression.

This is, after all, the main political question of our time, according to historian Timothy Snyder: what to do after empire? (Ukraine World 2024). The following reflections attempt to answer that question. More specifically, in a world where the 'post-colonial' is the predominant narrative and, at the same time, everything and everyone have been touched by colonialism to a greater or lesser extent, the praeter-colonial mind inquires 'if everything is pre-colonial, colonial, and post-colonial all at once, how can I make sense of it all?' As such, the praeter-colonial mind looks not for an apology or justification of all the evils of colonialism, but merely for an earnest explanation of colonialism's meaning and lasting impact on the present.

Roadmap

This book consists of the present Introduction, which makes up the remainder of this section; two main parts, Huddles and Struggles; and an Epilogue.

The first part, Huddles, refers to the groups or collectives we are often thrown into without further reflection and that we are expected to identify with. It will be divided into the following chapters, each of them corresponding to a separate online post: 1. The Grand Inquest of the World: British Imperialism and Europe; 2. The Reluctant Empire: The United States and America; 3. The Haves and the Have-nots: The West, the Global South, and the Rest; and 4. The Silicon Conquistadors: Humanity and Digital Colonialism in the Age of AI.

The second part, Struggles, addresses some of the main challenges of our tough times, regardless of the huddles we find ourselves being a part of. It is divided into the following chapters, also amounting to separate online posts: 5. The Colonial and its Discontents: Anti-Colonialism, Decolonization, and Post-Colonialism; 6. Existential Battles: Culture Wars and Real Wars; 7. Why We Fight: The Rules-Based International Order; 8. All Under Heaven: China's Awakening; and 9. America First, Humanity Second: Trump, MAGA, and American Imperialism Revisited.

The book that binds all of these chapters together is not meant to be read, necessarily, as a linear argument. Therefore, the reader can jump ahead and choose any of the above-mentioned chapters to start exercising the muscle of their praeter-colonial minds, with the exception of the Epilogue which I advise to leave for last. All the chapters, including this Introduction and the Epilogue, will be published as a stand-alone post online for easy access. It is likely that many readers will be drawn immediately to the chapters/posts that cover some of the most pressing issues of our time, such as, for instance, Chapter Nine on the MAGA movement and its neo-colonial implications, or Chapter Four on the perils AI poses for humanity and for self-determination. They are welcome to read those first or any that captures their attention. Each chapter will include references to the main theme of the book, namely the concept of the praeter-colonial that acts as the common thread cutting across all of them, to help the reader navigate all these intricate and complicated topics. Armed with this new concept of the praeter-colonial (which is defined and illustrated in the following sections), the reader might be able to better make sense of a post-colonial world where also the colonial and the pre-colonial coexist and compete as rationales in our everyday lives.

As this book is presented in various accessible formats, the reader can engage with it in different ways, and read it in whole or in part. But before you decide, allow me to continue with this Introduction which will provide an explanation of the purpose of this work, as well as a definition of the concept of the praeter-colonial and a rationale for this intellectual undertaking.

Vade Mecum (or a User Guide of sorts)

This is not a book about colonialism. At least not in the traditional sense, the way it is treated by scholars and politicians as a concept with one or two sharp edges, a word to cut through resistance of bodies and minds. Thus, this will not be a study about 'decolonization', 'anti-colonialism', 'post-colonialism', or any such trendy academic buzzwords, although some reckoning with these concepts will become necessary at some point.

Despite what the title may suggest, this book is not intended as a critique of colonialism or imperialism as such. It is an invitation for you to suspend your judgment about what all those things mean – insofar as such a proposition is even practicable when the very words you are reading right now are a legacy of colonialism, a testimony to the incredible soft power of one of the most successful colonial experiments in history, the British Empire.

In all honesty, English is not even my first language. But even if I tried to use my native tongue, Spanish, that would place us not very far removed from the epicenter whence English, and, at some point, Spanish, French, Dutch, and certainly the language lending a crucial prefix to this book's title, Latin, all come from. Thus, this will be in significant degree a book about Europe, and about Europeans.

Europeans are endlessly fascinating. Most of them offer a generous, unsolicited apology for their colonial past no sooner the topics of history or world politics come up. It is a nerve that does not even need to be struck, as the weight of the past keeps their hearts open in all their vibrance and vascularity. And for the most part, I believe their heart is in the right place when they do so.

However, I have yet to meet the European individual who, truly moved by historical guilt, vows to never leave their continent again. No, just as their forebearers, modern Europeans remain actively engaged with the world and in their travails of dissemination of the gospel they deem is the truth of the day, be it articulated in the language of 'trade', 'human rights', 'development', 'capacity building', and so on.

Of course, such a penitence would not solve any of the major problems of the world. It would probably make them worse, so interconnected our societies have become that they simply cannot afford to squander such a trove of human and financial resources as Europe. Still, it would be a remarkable thing if they entertained the thought if only for a moment. It would be nice of them to offer, and smart for the rest of us to gracefully decline.

But perhaps this is precisely what we need the idea of the praeter-colonial for – not to judge, nor to belittle or dismiss out of hand the efforts of thousands of honest, committed individuals whose only sin was to be born in the place where the so-called 'West' saw its first dawn. Thus, the concept of the praeter-colonial that is proposed in this study is one that remains neutral when facing the complicated legacy of colonialism. It does not judge, but it is an analytical tool to build judgment once we have come to terms with what our minds know and perhaps do not always articulate. It is not a guide to help people 'decolonize' their minds, partly because such an endeavor promises to prove futile, as the structures and legacies of imperialism are too entrenched, their roots running too deep in our forms of life to simply weed them out without losing something of our own selves in the process. As Yuval Noah Harari has eloquently put it: 'All human cultures are at least in part the legacy of empires and imperial civilisations, and no academic or political surgery can cut out the imperial legacies without killing the patient' (Harari 2014, 232). Thus, this is a book to help the mind take a step aside and have a long, hard look at its cultural make-up after half a millennium of colonial history.

This does not make this a psychological study. Nor is it an academic effort in the sense of being concerned primarily with engaging with the social sciences or humanities. There is no hypothesis to be proven or methodology to be applied. It is just a framework that the mind may use to converse with itself (Arendt 1976, 476), in order to find out what to it seems plausible or relatable even if no theorem, equation or scientific protocol can tell us why. It is a work of non-fiction to think about the fictions we carry within ourselves as scripts of sorts that we act out in our daily lives, whether we realize it or not.

Put more simply, this will be a collection of reflections for an age of contestation such as ours. It is an intellectual journey through the back alleys of empire that survive in the post-colonial era across some of those background concepts and ideas that are hidden behind the grandiose exteriors of civilization, democracy, freedom, human rights, self-determination, and the like. Not always suited for the foreground, these back alleys take the irregular form of irony, contradiction, discomfort, pain, and even injustice, all phenomena we must learn how to live with as we are in constant need of renegotiating the conditions making up the world around us. Even if we don't want to look at them, these back alleys remain an integral part of the entire structure that is our world.

A Brave New Word

Almost a decade ago a philosopher of science, Dr. Ruth E. Kastner, was inspired by a classic horror film to redefine the rather archaic term 'preternatural' as 'something at first disturbing and incomprehensible that nevertheless may become familiar and comprehensible once we better understand it through an expanded conceptual awareness' (Kastner 2016, para. 2). For example, magnets. The film titled 'The Haunting' (1963) features a researcher of the paranormal who tries to use science to understand phantasmagoric phenomena, thus turning it from 'supernatural' to 'preternatural' with the aid of logic and the scientific method. In a similar sense, I believe the concept of the 'praeter-colonial' can help us to approach colonialism and its legacies as something that, however disturbing and incomprehensible at first, may become familiar and comprehensible through the exercise of critical thinking that expands our conceptual and experiential awareness. The praeter-colonial mind, thus, seeks to acknowledge that the colonial is still with us even if we sometimes forget it or don't want to talk about it. As such, the praeter-colonial mind does not celebrate colonialism, but is ever mindful of its power.

'Praeter' is a Latin word that can mean 'past', 'by', 'beyond', 'above', 'more than', 'in addition to', or 'besides' (Oxford English Dictionary 2024). Hence, it will be the chief proposition of this study that the 'praeter-colonial' can mean all these things at once, namely 'the colonial as past', 'by or parallel to the colonial', 'beyond the colonial', 'above the colonial', 'more than the colonial', 'in addition to the colonial', or 'besides the colonial'. All these numerous possibilities enclose the risk that we may stretch the concept so thin that the expression 'praeter' becomes devoid of any meaning. In order to avoid this, the prefix must remain firmly anchored in the main concept it is attached to, or the 'colonial', much as the present cannot be really understood unless the colonial foundations it is built on are laid bare. Thus, as indicated above, the praeter-colonial mind is ever engaged in the intellectual task of trying to make sense of (i.e. making more comprehensible and familiar) a world that at some point has been either pre-colonial, colonial, or post-colonial, and the many ways in which this trajectory impacts the vantage point from which such task is undertaken, that is, the present. In other words, the mind that tries to make sense of all of this is the praeter-colonial mind, a mind that, in accordance with the varied meanings of the prefix 'praeter' (namely 'past, by, beyond, above, more than, in addition to, besides') sees colonialism simultaneously as past and present as it is confronted with the evidence of its many legacies. A mind that, in the end, attempts to step aside to gain perspective and go above and beyond colonialism for the sake of the present and the future.

Only our minds, as we think about all these possibilities, illuminated by our own experiences as individuals living in a world carved out by imperialism, can tell us whether these alternative meanings can make sense all of them at once, or only some of them, or none. Only our minds can demystify the 'supernatural', that is, the uncomfortably foreign within the colonial and turn it into the familiar and comprehensible 'praeter-colonial'. But perhaps a few examples may help in bringing down to earth all these abstract notions.

Jesus of Nazareth is perhaps one of the most salient examples of the praeter-colonial mind. He lived and died under the rule of one of the most powerful polities in history, the Roman Empire. He was versed not only in Hebrew and Aramaic from his homeland; he also spoke Greek and Latin, the two main languages of the empire. He learned a trade at the same time as he learned and mastered scripture. And he was not afraid to show his knowledge, and even to school those supposedly more erudite than him. But he was also someone who understood that the Roman Empire was not going to go anywhere anytime soon. He urged his followers to render unto Caesar the things that were Caesar's, for his kingdom was not of this world. He understood that some form of compromise was needed, 'the accommodation necessary to human as opposed to angelic life' (Carroll 2002, 115). Thus, his revolution of souls in a transcendent plane of existence (a post-colonial world of sorts) while the body remained beholden to the Romans was the very definition of the praeter-colonial.

Other exemplars of the praeter-colonial mind may be found besides the Son of man. One of the greatest pens of North America, John Steinbeck, writes in *East of Eden* that when the Spaniards arrived in the New World, they had to give everything they saw a new name – which was both a duty and a privilege (Steinbeck 1952). Yet, Steinbeck remains critical of their motives, as of those of American settlers after them. In the consecutive layers of conquest and empire that have covered North America, Steinbeck sees no clear claim for redemption, yet he understands perfectly well the succession of events and peoples that have given that part of the world its character, the same character that he portrays so uniquely.

Similarly, one of the greatest pens of South America, Gabriel García Márquez, writes in *One Hundred Years of Solitude* about a man facing the firing squad thinking back to the time when his father took him to see ice for the first time as a child (García Márquez 2017, 13), a rare material in the torrid tropical climate of the Amazon basin. The world was so new at the time, García Márquez continues, that many things were unnamed and they had to be pointed at to refer to them. Perhaps some of Steinbeck's explorers may have helped naming things that needed an identity. Or perhaps newcomers should have paid more attention to the way those who were there first referred to things. The point being, the waves of colonialism advancing north and south of the landmass known as America were relentless in their efforts to renew what they knew (or should have known) was old, ice standing as the ultimate metaphor of all things foreign (and northern) that were imported into those latitudes. Thus, both Steinbeck and García Márquez need the colonial to frame their narratives. That is, their praeter-colonial minds (and pens) need the colonial as the platform from where their stories may take flight and ultimately transcend, thus helping to shape national identities ('Americans', 'mestizos') that need to see themselves as both new to the soil they discovered/conquered and at the same time native to it in order to define their own character.

More examples can be found in other parts of the world. When asked what he thought about 'Western civilization', Gandhi reportedly said: 'It would be a good idea' (Tripathi 2004). He, too, can be thought of as an embodiment of the praeter-colonial mind as a harbinger of the post-colonial turning the tools of colonialism (such as law and philosophical argument) against it.

Another case may be found in one Turkish intellectual complaining about the fact that if he happens to do research in the West (say, Paris), everyone expects him to work on topics only related to religion or immigrants, not, for example, French urban planning (his actual calling) (Dikeç 2010). For him, being called 'Eurocentric' because he doesn't do 'identity research' is as ridiculous as trying to call his work in Paris 'field work' according to the academic metric that so divides the world.

Another example from Turkey is the writer Orhan Pamuk, who narrates in *The Black Book* how in a mannequin store the models no longer reflect the way real humans look and act because of the influence of Hollywood movies in society, as Turks no longer want to be Turks, they want to be something else (Pamuk 2011, 91–99). Thus, by aping gestures seen on screen, such as nods, winks, coughs, fits and the like, the citizens of Turkey – and of the world – have become uniform in their demeanor. Only a true praeter-colonial mind can denounce this imperial paradox afflicting a supposedly post-colonial world such as ours.

But popular culture also shows signs of true praeter-colonial spirit when, for example, a classic song like John Denver's *Country Roads* is adapted and reclaimed by a reggae band like Toots and the Maytals, who instead asked those roads to take them back home to West Jamaica, not West Virginia. There is a plasticity at work here that is a signature trait of the praeter-colonial mind as it can take the colonial and shape it or repurpose it, even reclaim it, as a display of agency and ownership.

The praeter-colonial can further be found in Georgia, a country that, like Ukraine, has seen much of human history unfold within its borders. Today, a popular American franchise, Wendy's, can be found all over the land. The franchise is owned by a business conglomerate that supports Russian influence in Georgia (the Wissol Group). At the same time, Chinese building companies have proliferated all over the Georgian landscape as they engage in the tireless construction of highways and tunnels as part of their 'One Belt One Road' initiative. Is Georgia, then, a truly post-colonial state?

In the field of defense, which owes a great debt to the developments of imperialism as we shall see in this book, another example of the praeter-colonial mind comes in the form of the code of ethics adopted by the New Zealand military, titled *The Way of the New Zealand Warrior* (New Zealand Army 2020). Therein, it is proudly claimed that the New Zealand professional of arms is a unique blend between the Māori warrior and the British soldier, both coexisting in harmony and enhancing each other's virtues and potential in one and the same 'kiwi at arms'.

Finally, some outstanding female figures can also be included among those displaying the praeter-colonial mind. Hannah Arendt, a German-Jewish philosopher who escaped Nazism, refused to be labeled as a victim or treated as a pawn in the chess game of great power competition during World War II. Displaying remarkable agency and analytical skill, she decided to stare evil in the eye to try and figure out how it could have grown such profound roots, in all its maleficence and banality, during the times of totalitarian rule in precisely the epicenter of civilization, Europe (Arendt 2006). It turns out that there is no guarantee against empire turning against itself and rearing its ugly head in the Homefront.

Another famous woman, Aung San Suu Kyi, a political activist who fought to gain democracy in Myanmar and won a Nobel Peace Prize for it, more recently has stood before the International Court of Justice to defend her country's use of genocidal violence against the Rohingya people, an unexpected move by a Nobel laureate coming from the 'Global South' and expected to be sympathetic to the cause of those oppressed by tyranny (Choudhury and Heiduk 2019). The complex and the paradoxical are also an integral part of the praeter-colonial mind, it would seem.

Many more examples from around the world can be included in this brief overview, but that is not necessary here, as there is no 'quota' to fill so that everyone is satisfied, or everyone is equally dissatisfied. These pages only tend to the intellectual need to stimulate the mind with a few illustrations that shall be paired with more anecdotal evidence and discussion throughout this study.

What all of the people mentioned above have in common is that they all understand that we live in a world that is shaped by empire and colonialism, a world where many things existed before empire and were so new they did not even have a name, and at the same time a world where pretty much everything (including these symbols your mind is currently decoding from English) is something that is a by-product of empire. But that is no reason not to try and go above and beyond the colonial, to reclaim it and give it new meaning to explain our shared experiences, to try and be more than and at the same time something in addition to the colonial tidings by which many, including ourselves, wish to define us.

So much for the purpose of this work and the meaning of the praeter-colonial. In the rest of this Introduction, I will delve into the rationale for undertaking this intellectual journey.

On the Road, An Intellectual Journey Begins

For me, it starts in Chile, where I was born and where I lived my entire life before moving to Europe. '*Chile?!*' The perplexity that descends upon the face of every single customs agent that is confronted with my passport is amusing at this point of my life. It happens every time, sometimes coupled with a smile, of the kind little kids draw on their faces when they learn that the colors they knew to exist can come together to form new tones and thus make their world richer without even having to pay for it. Or perhaps it is a nervous smile to mask their own ignorance. Some other times they double check with a colleague to see if they are reading the document correctly and to confirm whether we are friend or foe – the answer is invariably 'friend' because no one can think of a reason to call us the opposite. We are simply not that important. It always reminds me of a similar episode experienced by a Chilean traveler in Paris (in 1830, according to his memoirs), when a customs agent told him that his country did not exist, and that he must have come from Mexico, as there was no room in the European's mind for anything else in that side of the world. 'V. Perez Rosales, natural of Santiago of Mexico' the lie was proclaimed, printed and stamped to make it official (Pérez Rosales 1886, 100).

Even though Chile has existed as an independent nation at least since 1818 after almost a decade of military struggle against Spain, in the twenty-first century, same as in the nineteenth century, the sole proposition of such a place is still met with skepticism by the proper authorities. But we do exist. We have a flag and everything (as the British comedian Eddie Izzard has eloquently put it 'No flag, no country!'). Almost shaped like the Texas flag – even though we came up with ours twenty years before! – it also has the same colors, red, white and blue, which we adopted at a time when the

French revolution was still perceived as one of the greatest achievements in history, much as folks must have felt about the fledgling Soviet Union in the 1920s. We even adopted a quintessentially masonic, enlightened motto to go with the rest of our new republican regalia: *Post Tenebras Lux* or 'After the Darkness Comes the Light'.

It has become a great irony of history that my country's existence is doubted in the very place where nationhood and a right to exist as a nation are being defended every day as I write these lines, by a country whose existence an invader precisely denies out of imperialist aspirations. We must begin this study in such a place, where the pre-colonial, the colonial, and the post-colonial all converge and compete for purchase and validation. In a word, we must begin where there is fertile ground for the praeter-colonial mind to flourish. This story begins in Ukraine.

Ego Sum

'We exist! We exist!'. The words have never really been uttered by me when being controlled by border agents each time I go into Ukraine, although I have been tempted to shout them out in order to reassure them of the existence of my country – just as that Chilean traveler in Paris all those decades ago. This existential cry was written by Mykola Mikhnovsky, a Ukrainian lawyer and political activist living at the turn of the twentieth century, as he was making the case for an independent Ukraine finally free from the yoke of Russian imperialism (Mikhnovsky 1996, 213). One hundred twenty-five years later, these words remain as topical as the day when they were first written. It is indeed the battle cry of every Ukrainian man, woman and child, a nation up in arms fighting for its own survival. Indeed, Russia has been characterized as something the praeter-colonial mind may find not too difficult to understand, namely 'a postmodern empire, in which many of the physical features of empire have disappeared, but where the imperial spirit is still present and even resurgent' (Stent 2023, 180). Ukraine finds itself today at the receiving end of this resurgent imperialism.

But certainly, a country with its own flag, its own history and institutions, a full-fledged member of the United Nations, exists. Right? Or so we all thought, until Russian imperialists decided against it, calling Ukraine a made-up country. Of course, all states are artificial, as Jade McGlynn has pointed out (Lavrova 2024). It is not just Ukraine that had to be created. It is also the case with Russia, the United Kingdom, and every other country in the world, as countries are not found in a state of nature. In fact, they represent the next stage *after* human beings decide to congregate in order to transcend such a state of nature. The praeter-colonial mind understands that states are super-natural.

Further, this artificial quality is the very essence of a country that stands as one of the most successful experiments in self-government resulting from the ideals of the Enlightenment, the United States of America, a country that is not quite accurately defined as a nation, but as an idea – the proposition that all men are created equal, as we shall see in a later chapter. As Harari remarks in his latest book *Nexus*: 'There are no objective definitions for who is British, American, Norwegian, or Iraqi; all these identities are shaped by national and religious myths that are constantly challenged and revised' (Harari 2024, 29).

We must understand that this Enlightenment-inspired idea of equality stands as a challenge to everything humans had known so far, at least since the foundation of civil society, according to Jean-Jacques Rousseau, by 'The first man who, after enclosing a piece of ground, took it into his head to say, *this is mine*, and found people simple enough to believe him' (Rousseau 2022, 113).

Thus, the Enlightenment promoted the idea that, if inequality was brought about artificially by human beings when creating the first forms of political organization –empire being one of the oldest, most dominant ones throughout history (Kaplan 2023, 16) – then the remedy would also need to come artificially with the foundation of a new kind of body politic that would find a way to accommodate the often-times conflicting ideas of '*Liberté, égalité, fraternité'*. Enter the modern Nation-State, the product of a science of government so rational and universal it could be implemented anywhere in the world.

At least that is what you are told when you grow up in one of those 'made-up' countries Steinbeck and García Márquez write about, like the United States or Chile, those spawns of the Enlightenment found in places like the Western Hemisphere where we were promised that after the medieval *tenebras* the modern *lux* would come to light up our lives with the luminescence of the separation of powers, the rule of law and individual rights, with liberty and justice for all.

Certainly Europeans, of all people, will understand this. After all, Europe is where the Enlightenment first emerged, where these egalitarian ideals first took root. However, if Tocqueville was right and Americans have a passion for equality, then Europeans certainly have a soft spot, if not for inequality, at least for *difference*. Indeed, Europe gave us the problem (lack of natural equality) and the solution (more artificial equality through government) but somehow found a way to solve the former without deploying the latter. It seemingly got rid of inequality but kept differentiation (within itself and, even more strongly, against the rest of the world), while its current mélange of flags and institutions is something halfway between the colorful kaleidoscope of the feudal and the finite sepia shades of the imperial.

And all of this is precisely what Ukrainians want for themselves. They have so much need for the light after the darkness, for nationhood after servitude, that they are willing to pay the admission price every day with the blood of their sons and daughters. This is their (second) war of independence, and a lesson to the rest of us that no matter how certain you are of your own existence, you may at any point in history be required to reassert it with the words "I exist! I exist!".

Blood Will Tell

The blood being spilled right now in the battlefields and cities of Ukraine has sadly been poured generously over that part of the world in recent memory. Ukraine is located in what has been called the 'Bloodlands' by Timothy Snyder (Snyder 2015), by which he means the hapless space between two of the most blood-thirsty and tyrannical regimes in history, the Nazi and the Soviet empires. This area includes Ukraine, Poland, and the Baltic states. Whether by planned mass starvation, deportation, war, forced labor, or extermination, in the span of a few years the Bloodlands were irrigated with the lives of millions of human beings whose only crime was being born in the wrong side of the world, within the liminal space contained between two of the most conspicuous wrong sides of history.

When visiting the Bloodlands and reading about their dark history I must confess I succumbed to a form of stereotyping, whereby I was expecting to find dreary landscapes and crushed spirits everywhere. Like the 'green colonialists' of our time who want to preserve the landscapes of the so-called 'Global South' evergreen and virginal even at the expense of loss of revenue for local populations (Sanghera 2024, 103), I wanted to preserve the inhabitants of the Bloodlands perfectly still in a chrysalid made of their own dried tears. My mind was set to 'post-colonial' mode, we could say. I suppose it is similar to what happens to some visitors from across the pond when they go to Europe and expect everything to look and feel like a World War II movie. The fact that it was winter when I first visited the Bloodlands did not help things, the naked trees and grey skies making for an exquisitely foreboding aesthetic that would be the dream of any filmmaker in Hollywood.

But then, my prejudiced, post-colonial mind was challenged by the evidence it was confronted with. Yes, there were plenty of museums and monuments memorializing the sad events that took place in the Bloodlands, from the Holodomor Museum and Babyn Yar memorial in Kyiv to Auschwitz and the

Warsaw Rising Museum in Poland, as well as the KGB prison cells in Tallinn, the capital of Estonia. They all speak eloquently to the brutality those lands have seen.

At the same time, I was lucky enough to spend a Hallmark-worthy, snow-white Christmas in wartime Kyiv, enjoying comfortable beverages and plenty of good food at places that were open seven days a week and where electronic payment was a matter of course. In Warsaw, a city razed to the ground by World War II, I got to eat a cheeseburger in my swimsuit before entering one of the biggest spa centers I have seen in my life, complete with all kinds of saunas and facilities dedicated to wellbeing. And in Tallinn, where the USSR ruled with an iron fist even after Estonians gained their independence in 1920, I took a Bolt car across a city buzzing with activity to meet a friend to talk about his 'fintech' start-up business.

In a word, all these places strike one as vibrant, forward-looking societies where the memory of the dark events in the Bloodlands has not arrested their development in the slightest; on the contrary, it has strengthened their resolve to be the masters of their own destiny. In that sense, they have become the very definition of the praeter-colonial mind as they keep an eye on the past without it preventing them from looking ahead, into the future.

Great Expectations

If we zoom out from the Bloodlands and have a look at the wider universe of post-Soviet spaces a similar picture emerges. We are told by Hollywood (the same Hollywood that effectively re-engineered the way Turkish people carry themselves according to Pamuk's account) that post-Soviet spaces are bleak and depressing wastelands with no hope and no future. A travel log published by Michael Totten under the title *Where the West Ends* is a case in point (Totten 2012). The book describes this American writer's adventures in the Middle East, the Balkans, the Caucasus, and the Black Sea. Although Totten's wanderlust is nothing if not admirable, and mindful of the fact that the misadventures he recounts take place in a time when smart phones, simultaneous translation apps and GPS were a luxury as opposed to the household devices we take for granted in our daily lives today, one cannot but conclude that his views of those places are colored by the same type of post-colonial prejudice or stereotyping that afflicted me when I first ventured into the ominous Bloodlands.

It is not just Totten's constant complaining about how things are so different from back home (isn't that the point of traveling, anyway?), or the fatuous display of frustration at the impossibility to understand a language (and an alphabet) he did not study beforehand (I am just as ignorant as the next Westerner but I try not to complain too much and I manage to get by with whatever scintillations of Latin I can find hiding in foreign tongues). It is also his predisposition to continue to see that part of the world as a place where there is an objective deficit (a place that is lacking something we all need to sustain a life worth living), when in fact it is merely a place that stands in relative difference to what he knows – a place that simply does things differently to the West and were people manage just fine.

Totten concludes his account with a reflection inspired by what he deems a very depressing landscape on the shores of the Sea of Azov in eastern Ukraine:

> This place was so utterly godforsaken and misery-stricken I had a momentary feeling that the Union of Soviet Socialist Republics had never fallen apart, that, Mordor-like, its malice truly is sleepless, that it's still crushing parts of the world in its totalitarian fist (Ibid, Ch. 12).

And Totten is probably right about the lasting negative influence of Russian imperialism in that part of the world, where currently a war of independence is being fought precisely to resist that totalitarian fist.

However, having been more recently to many of those former Soviet spaces myself thanks to my wife's research and career – including Kazakhstan, Kyrgyzstan, Georgia, and Montenegro in addition to Ukraine, Poland, and Estonia – I believe that the same exhortation Snyder includes at the end of his book on the Bloodlands can be applicable to all those places in the world where people have been turned into numbers by tyrannical regimes. It is up to us to turn the numbers, and the stereotypes, back into real people (Snyder 2015, 408).

Thus, I have come to the informed conclusion, in exercising the faculties of a praeter-colonial mind illuminated by experience, that no place is forever cursed just because it was once ruled by an evil empire, and that we have no right to describe someone else's home as a corner of hell. What people want most of all in those places, and everywhere else, is to exercise agency, to receive respect, and ultimately to live with dignity.

Euro-Vision

If we zoom out even more and leave the post-Soviet spaces, we find the horizon to which Ukraine has aspired for at least a decade since the momentous Maidan protests of 2013-2014: Europe (hence the name 'Euro-Maidan'). Is Ukraine a part of Europe? When asking such a question, we need to be mindful of the fact that 'continents' and 'continental thinking' (like 'Europe' and 'Europeanness') had to be invented by someone (e.g. Greeks and Persians) (Quinn 2024, 225). Is Ukraine European? Can it be? Can it make its 'European decision' the same way Georgia has (Japaridze 2022, 50)? These are the questions that are killing thousands every day in Ukraine's war of independence, so we had better ponder their answers very carefully as we proceed.

A prominent contemporary Ukrainian historian, Serhii Plokhy, certainly seems to think so, calling Ukraine *The Gates of Europe* (Plokhy 2015), a quintessential borderland whose history is indissolubly linked to the history of Europe, as Ukraine has always been a gateway to the Old Continent as well as a bridge between Europe and Eurasia. Tracing Ukraine's early history back to Herodotus himself, Plokhy argues that it was the first frontier of the political and cultural sphere that began in ancient Greece and that we now call the West. Thus, Ukraine is 'where the West began to define itself and its other' (Ibid, 27). Furthermore, others argue, Ukraine's past, present and future are inextricably tied to the West (Kuleba 2021).

In all its rich history, ever interwoven with world events, it would be easy to see Ukraine as a mere clearing-house or a simple node in the circuitry of historical forces. Yet, it is so much more than that, as an impressive cast of characters left an indelible mark on the face of the country like so many layers of a cake into which all of them – Scythians, Sarmatians, Slavs, Jews, Khazars, Vikings, Mongols, Tatars, Cossacks, Poles, Lithuanians, Habsburgs, Russians, Soviets – are baked, making up a unique national identity.

This is precisely what makes finding the 'European' within Ukraine sometimes difficult, as it may be hidden under some of these many layers. But every once in a while it erupts like a force of nature that cannot be contained, like when a monk climbs up the bell tower of the church of Saint Michael to send a distress call at the sight of the invading Golden Horde in the thirteenth century; or when an entire nation congregates for months in the cold, open space of the Maidan (a word of Indo-European stock) to reclaim their rightful place in Herodotus's world in the twenty-first century. It can also be observed in the reappropriation of Virgil's *Aeneid* by a Ukrainian poet from the eighteenth century, Ivan Kotlyarevsky, at a critical time when the Cossack identity was struggling to survive consecutive imperial onslaughts coming from East and West (Kotlyarevsky 2004).

If, as one philosopher puts it, Europe's first word was 'rage' – as found in the opening act of Homer's *Illiad* (Sloterdijk 2010, 1) – then 'perseverance' is a concept that we may definitely draw from Virgil's epic tale of Trojan refugees founding the city of Rome, as well as from Kotlyarevsky's *Eneida* where Cossacks endure after the destruction of their polity by the Russian Empire. Rage may be Europe's first word, but perseverance is its creed, and Ukraine its paladin.

But perhaps the question we should be asking, by availing ourselves of the faculties of the praeter-colonial mind, is not 'Is Ukraine a part of Europe?', but the more fundamental inquiry 'What is Europe, anyway?'. If we consider that it is a place named after a Phoenician princess kidnapped by Zeus and taken away from her home in today's Lebanon, as the myth goes, then it would be fair to say that not even Europe is truly 'European'. What makes us say, then, that something or someone definitely count as a part of Europe? Will we know it when we see it? Or have we been conditioned to approach the question with a tunnel-vision that prevents us from seeing what may be right in front of us, only perhaps a little to the East, a little to the South?

One of such suspiciously meridional (or southern) places that have been at times stripped off their 'Europeanness' is the Iberian Peninsula. Even though in geographical terms it is a contiguous part of the landmass of the European continent, it is not always seen as a proper European country, or at least not a 'Western European' one. All Spain and Portugal can claim for themselves is the dubious title of 'Southern European', alongside other problem children such as Italy and Greece whose economies have needed in the past to be shored up or bailed out by their more solvent septentrional brethren.

In addition to the struggles of the present, Iberian countries are guilty of the mortal sin of not having stopped the Muslim advance in Europe in the eighth century – unlike their fabled Frank counterparts in Poitiers in 732. As a result, more than half of the Iberian Peninsula was occupied by Muslim invaders and turned into the land known as Al-Andalus – although an event spanning eight centuries and leaving indelible marks on the face and soul of all the peoples involved is somewhat mischaracterized by the use of the word 'occupation' and would probably be better described as a full-on colonization. It was not enough that the Catholic kings eventually rallied and managed to single-handedly expel the Muslims (and the Jews, for good measure) from their corner of Europe in 1492. It was already too late for Iberia to remain a 'pure' part of Europe as it had been 'contaminated' by centuries of Eastern influence in the eyes of the rest of Europeans, whom we know love a good opportunity to nurse their differences, that they may grow strong and hard to eradicate.

And so, a feeling of Hispanophobia started to take hold over the centuries (Roca 2020), which was only exacerbated by imperial rivalries whereby the

Dutch, the French, and the British were only too happy to contribute to the effort to taint the reputation of the Spanish Empire, around which a 'Black Legend' was built that spoke of the genocidal brutality of the *conquistadores* lusting after blood and gold wherever they went. I shall revisit this imperial whataboutism and its discontents in the following chapters. For now, the case of the Iberian Peninsula may serve as a litmus test to ascertain what counts as truly European, and thus it may provide a useful case study to address some of the struggles and challenges of the Ukrainian plight in the present.

Not unlike Ukraine, Iberia has been called home by many consecutive peoples throughout the ages, including Celts, Phoenicians, Greeks, Romans, Jews, Visigoths, and Muslims. The foundation of the Caliphate of Cordoba in Al-Andalus after the Muslim takeover did not amount to a dark age when all knowledge and culture were lost or fell through the cracks of history.

On the contrary, the city of Cordoba was called once a true 'Ornament of the World' (Menocal 2003), a beacon of progress in the otherwise dark Middle Ages, a place where religious tolerance was a way of life and where the troves of European and Middle Eastern culture were preserved and treasured as much as gold. It is in part thanks to such conservation efforts amidst this unique intellectual vibrancy resulting from centuries of Iberian *Convivencia* or 'coexistence' (Carroll 2002, 322–332) that we today can access the foundational texts of the European canon, including the contributions of Herodotus and Thucydides to history; of Hippocrates to medicine; of Archimedes and Ptolemy to science; and of Plato, Aristotle, Cicero, and Seneca to philosophy. Far from disappearing from the face of the earth, the European identity remained alive and well, among others, under the stewardship of the overlords of Al-Andalus and elsewhere in the Muslim world (Quinn 2024, 369-382).

Was medieval Iberia a part of Europe, then? Probably yes, if we measure it not only by its geography, but by its contributions to the preservation of European culture. Was medieval Ukraine a part of Europe? Also probably yes, for it at least represents what Plokhy calls the gate located at its easternmost part, just as Iberia may be called the gate of Europe's westernmost flank. Is Ukraine today entitled to full-fledge membership in the European family, like Spain and Portugal, despite of – or perhaps due to – its non-European influences?

Equipped with the sobering lessons of history, the praeter-colonial mind must ponder these questions critically and in earnest as it tries to assess the value of the past for the understanding of the present and the construction of the future.

Rockin' in the Free World

We may lastly try to zoom out even more in order to situate Europe within a wider geopolitical construct that is quite prevalent in the way we see and talk about the world today: the 'West'. I shall have more to say about the West and the rest in Chapter Three. For now, it is worth pointing out here that, as a construct or an idea, the West it is not quite geographically bound as, say, 'the Caribbean' or 'the Horn of Africa'.

The West encompasses not only most of Europe, but also significant parts of North America (including the US and Canada), as well as a myriad of distant, yet undoubtedly 'Western-like' polities, such as Australia, New Zealand, and arguably Japan. If we are being very generous – the way my teachers and elders were when I was growing up in Chile, telling me we also belonged in the West as we speak a European language, have European institutions and a European culture and life-style complete with a pervasive American influence – we may also include Latin America, although we would probably be met with skepticism and even amusement by Europeans, those masters of difference.

But what is it about the West that everyone wants a piece of it? What is the alure? The West looms large as a positive force in some of the most popular fictions of our time, including J.R.R. Tolkien's *Lord of the Rings* – where everything good and pure comes from the West, even beyond the sea, while evil dwells in the East – and George R.R. Martin's *Game of Thrones* – where all the relevant plot developments happen in the land of 'Westeros'.

Beyond the realm of fiction, the strong appeal that the brand 'West' enjoys becomes also painfully visible when we see Europeans competing for the label, as they desperately try to shake off more ignominious tags that have a bad rap, such as 'Eastern' European (Müller 2018), over which they will take anything – even 'Central'! – that will move them closer to the West and the North.

In the meantime, no one really wants to claim the 'South' as a source of pride, at least not for the right reasons – the wrong ones including such unfortunate propositions as the racist 'The South will rise again!' in the US, or the incredibly inaccurate 'Global South' at the international level. But if competition for the label 'West' is something that may cause the praeter-colonial mind to crack up in amusement, we must also bear in mind that right now there are people for whom accession to the coveted title is not only a matter of prestige or status: it may literally mean the difference between life and death, between the patronage and the protection of other members of the

West (in the form of military alliances such as NATO, or in the shape of political and economic communities that can have a measurable positive impact in the wellbeing of their members, like the European Union), and the continued oppression of their former colonial masters to the East. For Ukrainians, being called 'Eastern' instead of 'Western' is no joke if that places them closer to their aggressive Russian neighbor with all its neo-imperialistic tendencies. Ukraine may feel it belongs in the European family, but Russia's characteristically 'Eurasian' ambiguity towards Europe (Stent 2023, 65) is threatening to drag all of its neighbors down with it *ad noctum,* into the night of tyranny and underdevelopment.

When Ukrainians are deprived of the title of 'European' after so much of Europe's history has actually transpired in that frontier-land 'where utopias and dystopias collide' (Lasheras 2022, 62), irrigated with the blood of its own sons and daughters, it must feel like an insult or an inexcusable oversight, almost coterminous with the denial of their own existence as a nation, the 'European' being an integral component of such an existence.

As they try to fight their way out of the shadow of empire towards the light of self-determination in 'the hope that light can overcome darkness' (Kuleba 2024, 12), we would do well to remember that we all come from places that were once covered in darkness.

PART ONE:

HUDDLES

1

The Grand Inquest of the World: British Imperialism and Europe

As defined in the Introduction, the praeter-colonial mind tries to make sense of a post-colonial world where also the colonial and the pre-colonial coexist and compete as rationales in our everyday lives. Where to begin a journey of discovery whereby the praeter-colonial mind can start to fully exercise its faculties and critical capabilities? A place embodying one of the most recent and successful imperial experiments in history, where the exploits of colonialism are celebrated as well as its dividends jealously preserved, sounds like the proper setting to begin this quest. We must begin at the British Museum, located in the heart of London.

It is immediately upon entering the magnificent neo-classic palace that serves as the Museum's humble abode that we are introduced to a treasure from ancient times: the Rosetta Stone. I remember reading about it in my history books at school back in Chile. The very stone used by French archeologist Jean-François Champollion to decode the secrets of one of the most beguiling civilizations in history by using Greek as a vehicle between past and present. I never thought I would get the chance to see with my own eyes an artifact from ancient Egypt, unless I could somehow manage to go back in time. It turns out that museums are the next best thing to time-travel.

The Rosetta Stone is among the proudest possessions of the British Museum, which boasts an impressive Antiquity wing spanning from ancient Egypt to Greece and Rome, in addition to all the other collections covering pretty much every period in history and every corner of the earth – complete with a *Moai* or stone statue from Easter Island, a place that for some reason is under Chile's jurisdiction as we shall see in Chapter Three dedicated to the 'Global South'. In other words, the British Museum is replete with things that should not be there.

The Rosetta Stone is certainly not supposed to be there. I am not saying this to echo the all too familiar argument that the British Museum should return all its artifacts to the countries from where the British Empire looted them. This is something that has been formulated so many times that it has become a punchline, most exquisitely brought to us by comedian James Acaster, who imagines the Brits replying to the peoples asking for their property back: 'Sorry, you can't have it back. We are still looking at it!'.

What I mean when I say that the Rosetta Stone should not be in the British Museum is not that it belongs in Egypt, although it probably does. What I mean is that it may as well have ended up in Paris, the capital of yet another European empire, as it was 'discovered' by French troops occupying Egypt at the end of the eighteenth century. It was only after the British took over that part of the world that the Stone was finally sent to London, where it has sat comfortably since 1801 (The British Museum 2017).

It takes a lot of self-confidence to believe that an ancient treasure might be better preserved in your own country rather than in the place where it comes from. It takes even more to be convinced that, of all the available options, your country is the best possible destination. This is an aspect of British imperialism that I believe is not talked about enough. Sure, many Brits, same as many other Europeans, believe they are better than the rest of the world. But we can spot variations even among Europeans themselves, the smaller the difference the bigger the wedge it drives between relatives – what psychologists refer to as the 'narcissism of minor differences', like when you militantly resist the way they do things at your cousin's house just because they are slightly different from what you grew up with ('They make hot cocoa with water instead of milk – the horror!').

In this chapter I would like to reflect on how the British have embraced this narcissism of minor differences and taken it to the next level, as they have styled themselves as the keepers of their European brethren while practicing their own brand of colonialism. Inspired by this sense of relative superiority, they have pushed the idea that every other European colonial enterprise has been irredeemably flawed for a variety of reasons including the Black Legend of the Spanish *Conquista*, the protean terror of French absolutism turned revolution, the viciousness of the Dutch descendants known as the Boers, the sheer cruelty of the Belgians, the recalcitrant warmongering of the Germanic Reich(s), and the rampant tyranny of the Soviet experiment. The first huddle we will explore, then, corresponds to all those English-speaking nations that are a result of this particular iteration of European imperialism. The fact that we are able to critically approach it whilst using the language it bequeathed to us as a vehicle of said critique is a fascinating aspect of the praeter-colonial mind, insofar as we are trying to make sense of a post-colonial present by drawing on the tools of a colonial legacy.

A Soul-searching Nation

British exceptionalism is nothing new. The last time the entire world heard about it was not that long ago, when the UK decided to opt-out of the European Union in 2016 under the banner of 'Brexit'. That a country would voluntarily decide to leave an organization that so many other nations are fighting to join – some of them, like Ukraine, even having to pay with blood for their audacity – lays bare the unbridled sense of superiority of its people. It's like a rich family deciding to pull their kids out of one of the best schools in the county because they believe they can do better with just a private tutor, while scores of other families are still on the waiting list hoping for an opening next semester.

Brits have very little tolerance for external advice or control, and they try to keep foreign interference with their own affairs to a minimum – a courtesy the self-styled 'Global Britain' has not extended to the rest of the world, certainly. Sure, they finally managed to break free from the 'shackles' of the EU; but they still have to suffer European oversight in matters of human rights, as they remain part of the Council of Europe and its judicial organ, the European Court of Human Rights sitting in Strasbourg.

But that is as far as they will go. They will not take advice from anyone, not from other Europeans, and certainly not from outside of Europe. It was undoubtedly a moment of great hilarity when in 2008 Sri Lanka, a former British colony, suggested in a UN report that the UK 'consider holding a referendum on the desirability or otherwise of a written constitution, preferably republican, which includes a bill of rights' (UN Human Rights Council 2008). This cheeky proposition by one of its former colonies was met with deafening silence in subsequent reports filed by the British government.

No, it is usually Brits telling the rest of the world what to do, for which they have effectively weaponized one of their most salient political traditions: commissions of inquiry (Sanghera 2024, 197). Indeed, according to a report prepared by the House of Commons titled *Government by Inquiry*: 'The tradition of the public inquiry has become a pivotal part of public life in Britain, and a major instrument of accountability' (House of Commons 2005, 7). Accordingly, the main organ commissioning such investigations, Parliament, has ever been perceived as 'the grand inquest of the nation' (Ibid, 10). But since many of these inquiries had a scope greater than the nation itself as they were also concerned with what was going on in the colonies, we may dub the British Empire 'the grand inquest of the world'.

Indeed, commissions of inquiry were effectively used by the British Empire to gather information about its colonial possessions in places like Ireland, South Africa, Mauritius, Ceylon, and the West Indies (Laidlaw 2012; Johnson 1978). The main objective of these probes was to gather information in order to promote accountability, good governance and reform in faraway places where public scrutiny was not always possible. In addition, fears of 'imperial contagion' were a constant concern in British politics (Laidlaw 2012, 756) in the sense that what was done in the colonies could just as easily be done in the metropolis – a thesis fully unpacked by Hannah Arendt in *The Origins of Totalitarianism* when thinking about European imperialism as a precursor to the Holocaust (Arendt 1962).

The British legacy of government by inquiry can further be seen today in places like America and Oceania, where some remarkable exercises in soul-searching and self-reflection have been conducted in the context of the hapless 'Global War on Terror'. The 2014 US Senate report on the use of torture by CIA agents (US Senate 2014), and the 2020 Brereton report on war crimes committed by Australian special forces in Afghanistan (Australian Defence Force 2020) are two remarkable examples of this longstanding tradition.

That Is Not Done

Commissions of inquiry were used by the British Empire not only as a way of gathering information and promoting reform within its own jurisdiction. They were also used to tell other powers what to do with the populations located in their respective overseas territories. One of the few examples of an overall positive humanitarian intervention, that is, the use of military force to stop massive rights violations, took place in 1860 in the province of Syria then under Ottoman control. Shocked by the violence perpetrated against local Christian populations in Mount Lebanon and Damascus, France and the UK sent troops, with the Ottoman Empire's consent, to restore peace and order. In the aftermath, and true to form in the British imperial tradition, a commission of inquiry was set up to determine responsibilities for the violence (Rodogno 2011, 181–182).

Perhaps one of the best examples of a commission of inquiry established by the British Empire to oversee the situation in the territories under control of another European power was the investigation leading up to what became known as the *Casement Report* (Louis 1964). Published in 1904 by Roger

Casement, the report contained an account of widespread acts of violence and brutality committed by Belgian and other European agents against native populations in what was known then as the Congo Free State, that is, the part of Congo colonized by King Leopold II of Belgium as his own private property.

The report, in which Casement vocally preached 'the gospel of Congo reform' (Ibid, 120), caused such an impact in European society at the time that it is said to have precipitated the end of the Congo Free State as a royal possession when it was turned into an official Belgian colony in 1908 – a modest slice of the African *gâteau* that the Belgians would hold on to for a further 52 years.

This and other accounts of the heinous acts of violence and outrageous abuses committed in the Belgian Congo inspired some of the most insightful works of fiction written about imperialism: *An Outpost of Progress* in 1897 (Conrad 2002a) and *Heart of Darkness* in 1899 (Conrad 2002b), both authored by Joseph Conrad, a Polish-British writer born in Ukraine.

Conrad's own position about imperialism remained ambiguous and nuanced, his praeter-colonial mind being able to accommodate both earnest praise for the advancement of 'light' and progress as well as sober condemnation of the horrendous assaults on humanity he witnessed. In his own words:

> The conquest of the earth, which mostly means the taking it away from those who have a different complexion or slightly flatter noses than ourselves, is not a pretty thing when you look into it too much. What redeems it is the idea only. An idea at the back of it; not a sentimental pretence but an idea (Ibid, 107).

Another remarkable European individual caught in the middle of the imperialist fever, whose exploits were immortalized by the late Peruvian writer and Nobel laureate Mario Vargas Llosa in his 2010 novel *El sueño del celta* (*The Dream of the Celt*) (Vargas Llosa 2010), is no other than the author of the Congo report: Roger Casement. If anyone epitomizes the spirit of the praeter-colonial mind at the turn of the twentieth century it is undoubtedly Casement.

Roger Casement was the poster child of the British fondness for commissions of inquiry. He was appointed by the UK government in 1903 to write his famous report on the Congo, as he happened to be the British consul in Boma at the time. After the success of this first inquiry, he was again commissioned by the Foreign Office to conduct an investigation on abuses committed against native workers collecting rubber for the UK-registered Peruvian Amazon Company. His two subsequent reports submitted in 1910–1911 were as damning as the Congo one, the colonial exploitation in South America striking him as brutal and unchecked as the one he documented in Africa. As a result of his inquest endeavors for the British Crown, he was knighted and became known henceforth as Sir Roger Casement.

But that is not the whole story. Although he was a subject of the British Crown, Sir Roger was in fact an Irishman born in Dublin. Being exposed to the darkest side of European imperialism in Africa and South America did not leave him untouched or particularly amenable to the footprint of colonialism much closer to home. His critical spirit and inquisitive expertise eventually, perhaps inevitably, led him to turn the gaze inwards and unveil what was in front of his eyes: British imperialism was incompatible with a sovereign and independent Ireland.

Thus, Casement secretly became an activist for the republican cause and plotted with the Germans during World War I to arm the Irish rebels on the eve of the Easter Rising of 1916. Upon landing in Kerry inside a German submarine, he was captured and tried for treason against the British Crown. His defense famously riding on a comma from an obscure medieval statute (Anderson 2013), and despite pleads for mercy coming from the likes of Sir Arthur Conan Doyle, W.B. Yeats and George Bernard Shaw (but not Conrad, who never forgave him his treachery), Casement was eventually convicted and hanged as a traitor on the third day of August, 1916.

Thus passed one of the great praeter-colonial minds of the long nineteenth century – a very complicated individual caught in the middle of a very complicated age. In his mind the duties of benign imperialism coexisted with a powerful drive for human decency and an increasingly strong yearn for freedom. The very tools of empire put at Casement's disposal to call out the depravity of other Europeans abroad led him to turn against the hypocrisy of his own masters and, ultimately, to his own demise.

Post-Imperial Hangover

Another remarkable praeter-colonial mind found in the British Isles today is Sathnam Sanghera, an English journalist author of the recent bestsellers *Empireland: How Imperialism Has Shaped Modern Britain* (Sanghera 2021), and *Empireworld: How British Imperialism Has Shaped the Globe* (Sanghera 2024).

Born to Indian Punjabi parents in the Midlands, and Cambridge educated, Sanghera is the personification of the 'British Dream' so many immigrants pursue when they decide to move to the UK. But he is so much more than that.

Incredibly insightful and self-aware to a fault, Sanghera represents one of the finest examples of the praeter-colonial mindset that is the topic of this study. His relationship with empire is complicated, not unlike other British liberals before him. For example, George Orwell understood very well the injustices the British Empire was built upon but was nonetheless not ready to give it all up lest this may 'reduce England to a cold and unimportant little island where we should all have to work very hard and live mainly on herrings and potatoes' (Zakaria 2024, 140), A.K.A. pre-industrial, pre-imperial England.

Sanghera begins *Empireland* by proposing the creation of a new holiday in Britain: 'Empire Awareness Day', or as he also calls it, 'Empire Day 2.0' (in reference to the traditional Empire Day that existed between 1916 and 1958). By remembering such a day, British people could better understand the many ways the concept of empire shapes their lives today, including Sanghera's (and so many others') own immigrant background:

> Empire explains why we have a diaspora of millions of Britons spread around the world. Empire explains the global pretensions of our Foreign and Defence secretaries. Empire explains the feeling that we are exceptional and can go it alone when it comes to everything from Brexit to dealing with global pandemics. Empire helped to establish the position of the City of London as one of the world's major financial centres, and also ensures that the interests of finance trump the interests of so many other groups in the twenty-first century. Empire explains how some of our richest families and institutions and cities became wealthy. Empire explains our particular brand of racism, it explains our distrust of cleverness, our propensity for jingoism. Let's face it, imperialism is not something that can be erased with a few statues being torn down or a few institutions facing up to their dark pasts; it exists as a legacy in my very being and, more widely, explains nothing less than who we are as a nation (Sanghera 2021, 26).

He further develops the point in *Empireworld,* where he argues that the fashionable concept of 'decolonization', although important for restoring the self-respect and agency of the formerly colonized, can only ever be 'tokenistic', as 'British imperialism is baked into our world and, frankly, it would be easier to take the ghee out of the masala omelettes I've become addicted to eating for breakfast in India' (Sanghera 2024, 18).

Sanghera is further skeptical of approaching the legacies of British imperialism with a 'balance sheet' view whereby it is sustained that, on balance, after pondering its evils versus its contributions, British colonialism is qualified either as relatively good (for example, under the inquest of the world narrative developed in this chapter) or relatively bad (eliciting feelings of guilt or shame, when in actuality, he writes, history doesn't care about anyone's feelings) (Ibid, 145).

The author believes that this nuance-free balance sheet approach, so common in today's culture wars, actually obscures what is an incredibly complicated and admittedly contradictory legacy that is ingrained in everything we do and everything we are today, and that engaging in a game of counterfactuals where we remove every imperial footprint from our world is simply unhelpful (Ibid, 282).

Another interesting point raised by Sanghera is what amounts to a rare and compelling exercise in historical humility, when he suggests that a reckoning with their imperial past would allow British people to be better prepared when the time comes for one or many of these formerly subjugated peoples to determine the former's destiny:

> There are other good reasons for Britons to understand this imperial history, and other imperial histories we've touched upon so far. When it comes to India, we need to appreciate its version of events because it's a burgeoning superpower that will shape our future in all sorts of ways, and we can't assume, as we've tended to, that they're nostalgic for a time they're actually trying to decolonize out of their system (Ibid, 145).

Ultimately, what Sanghera aims to achieve is to engage his countrymen and countrywomen so they, in turn, can join the ongoing dialogue about the legacies of imperialism that is already happening in the rest of the world, such that Brits can also assess and appreciate the highly complex reality of our present. 'This dialogue would allow us to live in an infinitely more sophisticated, more interesting world' (Ibid, 68) he concludes, adding that the ability to identify contradictory legacies and learning to live with them can actually be liberating. Because of what he writes, and because of what he is (how could we separate the two?), Sanghera is the archetypal prater-colonial mind of twenty-first century Britain.

We Need More British Museums

In the late 1990s Michael Ignatieff observed that there were some 'Conradian continuities' between the many humanitarian and military international engagements led by the West at the time and the classical interventionism of the age of empire (Ignatieff 1998, 93). He was referring to Joseph Conrad, an author we already mentioned here, whose name has become synonym with the awareness and denunciation of the excesses of colonialism.

Yet, as I also mentioned before, Conrad's position on colonialism is at best nuanced, even praeter-colonial, as he believed in the possibility to redeem all the suffering with an idea, namely the notion that the light of civilization can make the darkness recede – unless, of course, the heart of darkness nests within all of us, a possibility he also seems to entertain when the narrator of *Heart of Darkness,* Marlow, experiences a sense of 'remote kinship' with the wild and passionate uproar coming from the men dwelling in the night of first ages (Conrad 2002b, 139; Maier-Katkin and Maier-Katkin 2004).

Conrad's own praeter-colonial approach is best illustrated at the beginning of *Heart of Darkness,* when the narrator contemplates the Thames at dusk and suddenly declares that London, that beacon of civilization, the very heart of empire at the turn of the twentieth century, has also been 'one of the dark places of the earth' (Conrad 2002b, 105). By that he means that, a long time ago, when the first Roman triremes were making their way upstream over 'a sea the colour of lead' under 'a sky the colour of smoke', venturing into the unknown in this remote outpost of the Roman Empire, that part of the world was also deprived of all the things we consider a part of progress and civilization – law, order, commerce, industry, prosperity, and peace. In a word, the light, whose luminescence had to be carried to this 'poor backwater' (Acemoglu and Robinson 2012, 174) by the conquerors (Conrad 2002a, 9; Lindqvist 2018, 11–27). In that sense, the British Empire learned from the very best.

I thought of all these things as I walked through the streets of London, a place I once called home when I was a doctoral candidate. When I visited the British Museum for the first time, I suddenly found my post-colonial mind resenting this formerly dark place of the earth that believes it can now house ancient treasures and wonders from all over the world just because they were captured by force, not least an artifact, the *Moai,* that my own compatriots want back, even if the Brits are still looking at it.

But then I saw it: It was a Sunday morning, and families were out and about. They had taken their children to visit this admission-free museum so they could learn all about ancient Egypt, Greece, Rome, the Middle Ages, China, India, America, and even a place as remote as Easter Island. As I saw kids observing all these wonders of history, absorbing every detail in their developing brains, I couldn't help but think how rich their education was turning out to be, how many secrets of this world they could access and how much better versions of themselves they would grow up to be just by being exposed to such a treasure trove of human knowledge. And then it hit me, as my prejudiced post-colonial mind gave way to a more nuanced prater-colonial thought: We don't need to get rid of the British Museum. What we need is more British Museums around the world, where kids of all places can access this kind of knowledge in their own towns. I imagine a worldwide network of museums sharing these artifacts so we can give every kid the opportunity to access a high-quality education. The practical details would need to be sorted out, of course, as many objects would not be able to be so easily transported back and forth. But they did transport them back in the day when conservation technology was not as advanced. We can do it again, more fairly this time, thus making sure children everywhere in the world can be amazed by the treasures of humankind, that their little praeter-colonial minds may grow strong and wise.

2

The Reluctant Empire: The United States and America

'What kind of American are you?' is a line from the 2024 movie *Civil War.* It will hit Latin Americans in a particularly powerful way – as one of the stars of the film, Wagner Moura, admitted during an interview when asked about the scene in which his character is confronted with a trigger-happy militia man with a keen interest in geography and demographics:

> 'What kind of American are you' is something that really strikes me, as someone that is not from here. I'm an American citizen, too, but I speak with an accent and I'm Brazilian. (...) In the end, when we wrapped, really, I laid down in the grass and cried for 15 minutes. It says something about being a Latino in this country, and it was a really strong scene for me (Weintraub and Jones 2024, para. 27).

Coming out of the movie theater after watching the new blockbuster, the same question kept popping up in my head. I am definitely not the right kind of American in the eyes of the murderous inquisitor, and if I were in that situation, admitting I come from Chile would have bought me a one-way ticket to the mass grave where the one guy from Hong Kong also ends up. I am a Latino, and I have also been a Latino in that country, just like Moura. And although I am not a citizen, I am technically *American*, because I was born in the continent bearing that name. There are many peoples and many states scattered across that gigantic landmass stretching from Alaska to Tierra del Fuego. Some of them are united, some divided. But they are all American.

It feels only natural to dovetail our reflections on the British Empire with a chapter dedicated to one of the most salient continuations of the imperial experience coming out of Merry Old England: the United States of America. This is a point only made incidentally by Sathnam Sanghera when he underscores that the US is a British imperial creation, and that 'One of the biggest lies America tells itself is that it rejects everything the awful [British] empire ever stood for' (Sanghera 2024, 23). In this chapter I would like to pay more attention to this sprout of British imperialism to explore how the praeter-colonial mind can make sense of what I call the 'Reluctant Empire' – an empire in all but name in a supposedly post-colonial era. Since this is a chapter on the community of nations that is, or should be, known collectively as 'Americans' – that is, the inhabitants of the continent of America – it belongs in the first part of this study dedicated to all these different 'Huddles' we choose, or are made, to identify with. A separate chapter, titled 'America First, Humanity Second: Trump, MAGA, and American Imperialism Revisited' (Chapter Nine), will further delve into the many challenges that neo-imperial Trumpism poses to the world, and particular the Americas. I advise the reader to use that chapter as a companion to the present one.

We Are All Americans

When I was a teenager growing up in Chile in the 2000s, for some reason it became fashionable to be anti-American – a fad that occasionally afflicts Europeans and Latin Americans alike. In this iteration I witnessed how some of my classmates who just a few years before enjoyed the latest episodes of Friends, The Simpsons, or WWE, and listened to music released by Green Day, The Red Hot Chili Peppers, or Blink 182, overnight started hating the US and rejecting everything it stood for.

Some of them even formed a band called Yanquis Muertos ('Dead Yankees'), such was the extent of their new-found resentment. I can still hear the lyrics of their first ever single, played to the tune of a reasonably good punk rock track: '¡No queremos más yanquis, yanquis!' ('We don't want any more Yankees, Yankees!'). The lead guitarist would make comments such as 'They don't even have a proper name – the US is a country without a name', meaning that all the words 'United States of America' convey is a form of political organization plus a geographic location, or 'an adjective attached to a generic noun' (Grandin 2025, xxi). How the similar designation 'United Kingdom of Great Britain and Northern Ireland' slipped under his radar is beyond me.

However, there is a point to the traditional objection against the use of the term 'America' to refer to a single country in a continent housing three dozen different nations (Rousseau and Houdart 2007). Every person located south of the Río Bravo will scold you if you use 'America' to signify the US, or 'American' to refer to its citizens. 'We are all American – America is a continent' the bitter retort will usually go.

And it is technically correct. America is indeed a continent, named almost by accident by a German cartographer in 1507, Martin Waldseemüller, who drew up the first world map designating the continent 'discovered' by Columbus as 'America', in recognition of the exploits of one Amerigo Vespucci, an Italian sailor who circumnavigated the globe and thus confirmed that the territory Columbus thought was India was indeed a separate continent (Parker 2022, 93).

If you think about it, the new landmass might just as well have been named 'Vespucia' instead of 'America', and the country that is the subject of this chapter would be called the 'United States of Vespucia', populated by Vespucians living the Vespucian Dream, all the while Latinos insisting that we are all indeed Vespucians. Or, if history was a little fairer, the continent would be named after Columbus, thus 'Columbia' not amounting to just a university in New York or 'Colombia' to one single country in South America (Grandin 2025, xv). William Thornton, the designer of the Capitol building in Washington D.C., thought as much when he proposed his idea for a Pan-American Constitution for 'United North and South Columbia' in 1800 (Andrew et al. 1932).

Doesn't Columbus deserve a continent with his name on it to match the magnitude of this contribution to world history, for better or worse? But history is rarely fair or accurate like that, so America it is and America it will remain. Not surprisingly, Waldseemüller's map containing what has been called the 'birth certificate' of America sits in the Library of the US Congress after the North American country paid handsomely to acquire such a precious – arguably the very first – piece of Americana.

'Hacerse la América'

America is, thus, a place. But not just any place. According to aggregated demographic trends over the past five hundred years, it would appear that it is *the* place to be – not just the North, and in particular the United States, but the entire continent brimming with potential and opportunity in the eyes of Europeans and other peoples, hence the Spanish expression '*Hacerse la América*', the closest translation of which would be 'to make America happen for you'. In that sense, America is not just a place, even one as beautiful as to confront the traveler from distant lands with 'something commensurate to his capacity for wonder' (Scott Fitzgerald 2001, 151) to borrow a line from *The Great Gatsby*. America is not merely a place, but a concept, an idea. What idea is that?

Alexis de Tocqueville, the French thinker who authored one of the most insightful x-rays ever taken of the young North American body politic of the early nineteenth century, observed about democratic (as opposed to aristocratic) peoples that they 'have a natural taste for freedom: left to themselves, they will seek it, cherish it, and view any privation of it with regret'. Yet, Tocqueville concludes that 'for equality, their passion is ardent, insatiable, incessant, invincible' (Tocqueville 2009, 962).

Despite some critical factors sometimes obscuring it – not least recalcitrant racial, gender and income inequality – this passion for equality can be observed in every detail of American life, from its signature first-name-basis treatment to the mass-produced uniformity of its economic life, from the political balance of its perfectly symmetrical Senate (100 seats, 2 for each of the 50 states) to the deeply held belief that all men are created equal in 'a nation bound together not by ties of blood or religion, but by paper and ink' (Rivkin and Casey 2001, 35–36).

This passion for equality is also the main driver behind the strong political commitment to merit that is characteristic of the US – flawed and non-factual as it may be sometimes. One of the most American characters I have ever met in my life is actually a man from Kyrgyzstan who works in tech and is actively involved in an outlandish political project he described as 'Meritland', a collection of like-minded, hardworking individuals planning to start their own country, a tech-utopia open to all those willing to take a skills test to join. They are even looking for real estate opportunities around the world to bring their vision into life. He may or may not have actually been to the US, and his peculiar dream may never come to fruition, but to me this Kyrgyz man seemed as American as apple pie or Jay Gatsby, who, according to F. Scott Fitzgerald, believed in that metaphorical green light representing a future 'that year by year recedes before us. It eluded us then, but that's no matter – to-morrow we will run faster, stretch out our arms farther…And one fine morning –' (Scott Fitzgerald 2001, 151).

The Reluctant Empire

After hurricane Maria struck Puerto Rico in 2017, President Donald Trump delivered the following message to its distraught population: 'I hate to tell you, Puerto Rico, but you've thrown our budget a little out of whack, because we've spent a lot of money on Puerto Rico and that's fine, we've saved a lot of lives' (CNN 2017, para. 6). What was he even doing there? Puerto Rico is not a state of the US. But it does have a special relationship with the North American country. Technically, Puerto Rico is an unincorporated territory of the United States, falling under the jurisdiction of the US Congress. Some may even say Puerto Rico is a colony of sorts. It was gained by the US after it defeated Spain in 1898, a conflict that also resulted in the acquisition of Guam and the Philippines for the North American country, as well as a strong presence in Cuba that remains effective today in Guantánamo Bay.

Just like the Athenians brazenly declared to the inhabitants of the island of Melos during the Peloponnesian War that 'the strong do what they will while the weak suffer what they must', the US of the turn of the twentieth century did with all these islands as it pleased and they had to suffer it, thus affording Donald Trump the chance to show up there a century later and talk to their inhabitants as a rent collector. But saying that Puerto Rico is a colony of sorts would entail that the US is an empire of sorts. Is it though?

If the US is an empire today then its origin story must be found in its predecessor, the British Empire. But however much Americans love to portray Brits as villains in every narrative, as Sanghera also reminds us (Sanghera 2024, 28), the British Empire was not in actuality a product of pure evil or a criminal masterplan of world domination. It may not even have been deliberate to begin with. Through the sheer power of private capital backed by brute force, the British expanded their influence across the globe, more for profit than for anything else. Eventually, they found themselves in possession of a vast network of colonial outposts owned by subjects of the same sovereign, such as the East India Company or the West India Company, and presto: British Empire. It was an empire 'acquired in a fit of absence of mind' (Sanghera 2021, 42), an 'inadvertent empire' (Roca 2020, 53).

If in the end the British fully embraced their imperial identity and even named some of their most famous institutions after it – as evidenced by such relics as the Imperial College London or the Imperial War Museum – Americans, on the other hand, have a hard time accepting their legacy – Donald Trump's neo-imperialistic designs notwithstanding, about which I will have more to say in Chapter Nine.

We may even say that often times Americans display a post-colonial mindset, as they proudly broke free from the evil empire; but, at the same time, they behave in a way that would be better understood from a praeter-colonial point of view, with all its complexities and contradictions – wishing they could have their imperial cake and eat it too, as it were. Like Michael Ignatieff says: 'Americans have had an empire since Teddy Roosevelt yet persist in believing they do not' (Ignatieff 2003, 1). This empire in denial can indeed be called the 'Reluctant Empire', paraphrasing Teddy Roosevelt's remark about how the US might at times have to, 'however reluctantly' (Allison 2017, 239), step in to enforce the Monroe Doctrine. Crucially, the emperor's reluctance to rule means that sometimes lesser kings may and will come out to play (Lévy, 2019).

The Reluctant Empire is different from its European predecessors in that, although it has perfected the informal exercise of power they invented, through private initiative and the free movement of capital and people around the world (Koskenniemi 2011, 35–36), it refuses to embrace its true nature as an empire. This may stem from the fact that the methods to expand its influence often come not in the form of hard power (of which, for sure, it also has plenty), but as incredibly effective and irresistible displays of soft power ranging from the opening of Coca-Cola factories and Rotary Club branches to the expansion of a form of hegemony without formal colonies (De Grazia 2006). In other words, 'a global sphere of influence without the burden of direct administration and the risks of daily policing' (Ignatieff 2003, 2). Precisely the same kind of soft power based on 'attraction' that the second Trump administration is squandering at an alarming rate (Keohane and Nye 2025), as we shall see in Chapter Nine.

Furthermore, this Reluctant Empire styles itself as the champion of freedom, democracy and human rights around the world, because all these values espoused by the 'humanitarian empire' (Ignatieff 2003, 17) are held to be self-evident, that is, natural or universal truths that can and must be accepted by all, as inevitably as accepting that two plus two equals four. And if you are disseminating the word of what is true and universal, what should be grasped intuitively by the human mind wherever it may be found while history is 'suspended' as a result of this immutability (Hardt and Negri 2000, xiv), how can you think of yourself as imposing anything? How could you not see your project as one of liberation whereby the truth within every human being is unlocked and their potential unleashed?

The Indigenous American Berserk

The main problem with this schizophrenic post-colonial/colonialist mindset is that it is not sustainable as it does not measure up to the challenges of our age, as we shall also see in Chapter Nine. Americans want their hegemony, but they don't want to commit too much blood and treasure to maintaining it. They see a humanitarian catastrophe and haste to help those in need. But then they haste back, riding off into the sunset after their work is done. They 'feed and leave', because they 'lack the imperial cast of mind' (Ferguson 2004, 29), as well as that illusion of permanence that is the essence of successful imperialism (Kaplan 2023, 258). As Ignatieff puts it:

> These new empires depend, ultimately, on the staying power of electorates, and democratic peoples make fickle imperialists. (...) But empires don't come lite. They come heavy, or they do not last (Ignatieff 2003, 116).

As with every empire built on the foundation of democratic institutions, then, the main challenges and dangers for the American empire come not from foreign competitors, but from within. Tocqueville's account of America's passion for equality already contained a warning, all those centuries ago:

> they call for equality in freedom; and if they cannot obtain that, they still call for equality in slavery. They will endure poverty, servitude, barbarism – but they will not endure aristocracy. This is true at all times, and especially true in our own (Tocqueville 2009, 962).

Tocqueville further calls our attention to the perils of individualism, which is a more sophisticated version of egotism unique to democratic societies:

> Individualism is a mature and calm feeling, which disposes each member of the community to sever himself from the mass of his fellow-creatures; and to draw apart with his family and his friends; so that, after he has thus formed a little circle of his own, he willingly leaves society at large to itself.
>
> (…)
>
> Aristocracy had made a chain of all the members of the community, from the peasant to the king: democracy breaks that chain, and severs every link of it (…). Thus not only does democracy make every man forget his ancestors, but it hides his descendants, and separates his contemporaries from him; it throws him back forever upon himself alone, and threatens in the end to confine him entirely within the solitude of his own heart (Ibid, 963; 965–966).

Is it any wonder that an empire with such a societal makeup will lack appetite for foreign adventures and long-term global commitments, when its citizens show no interest in what goes on beyond their own parochial reality?

And it can get worse. If Americans (or any democratic society, for that matter), retire from public life and surrender it to less than qualified individuals (the consequences of which we will explore in Chapter Nine), then John Adam's additional warning to his youngest son, Thomas, will always come back to haunt them: 'Public business my son, must always be done by somebody – it will be done by somebody or other— If wise men decline it others will not: if honest men refuse it, others will not' (Adams 1789, para. 1). Thus, the rule of unwise, dishonest characters over millions of disinterested individuals can only end badly for everyone involved – both within and outside their borders. The warning signs are all there, the writing on the wall found not only in the words bequeathed to us by great political thinkers, but also in works of fiction. It can be seen, for instance, in the new *Civil War* movie that opened this chapter, portraying a very plausible scenario of internecine political confrontation in an already divided America.

It can also be found in the pen of a great American writer, Philip Roth. In *The Plot Against America* he imagines what would have happened in the US if the fascist candidate had won the presidential election of 1940. The outcome is not hard to predict: America never enters the war and antisemitism runs amok. Amidst all the darkness of this story, which we can comfortably assess from the light that the 'right side of history' sheds upon us, Roth presents us with a sobering reminder: 'The terror of the unforeseen is what the science of history hides, turning a disaster into an epic' (Roth 2005, 113–114). In *American Pastoral* Roth also warns us about the dormant demon of political violence that dwells within, the antithesis of the idyllic American Dream: the counter-pastoral of the 'indigenous American berserk' (Roth 1998, 92).

This germ of political violence is, of course, not only indigenous to North America, nor can it be identified with any particular group. It is just raw humanity, human nature at its most primeval, the inherent heart of darkness Conrad wrote about when contemplating the checkered record of civilization in his day. It was likewise experienced firsthand by another (South) American, one of Argentina's founding fathers, Francisco Narciso de Laprida, who tried to establish the rule of law in his young nation only to arrive at a crude awakening to the minotaur-like dream that was the Spanish Empire, half humanist, half beast (Grandin 2025, 182). Doctor Laprida's last thoughts before being executed by political rivals would be famously conjectured by the poet Jorge Luis Borges over a century later:

> I who wished to be someone else, to be a man of judgments,
> of books, of rulings, I shall lie in the mud under open skies; but
> a secret joy inexplicably elates my chest. At last, I meet my
> South American destiny (Borges 1943).

Will the US ever have to meet its North American destiny? Will it embrace it with equal joy?

Give Me Your Bad Hombres

What kind of American was our ill-fated Laprida? A son of Argentina educated in Chile, he seems to be an American of the Southern variety. He would have definitely met his North American destiny in the *Civil War* movie, landing next to me and the Hong Kong guy in the mass grave, as he is the kind of 'bad hombre' that features in the nightmares of many conservative Americans dreading an influx of the worst elements of society pushing through the southern border. Isn't that kind of the point of America (the country and the continent) though? Isn't a faith in the redeeming power of the New World, making America 'more an ideal than a place' (Grandin 2025, xix), the main driver behind every revolution from New England to Patagonia?

In the poem inscribed at the feet of the Statue of Liberty, *The New Colossus* by Emma Lazarus, this quintessential American symbol, 'Mother of Exiles', casts a message to the Old World:

> Keep, ancient lands, your storied pomp! (…) Give me your tired, your poor, your huddled masses yearning to breathe free, the wretched refuse of your teeming shore. Send these, the homeless, tempest-tost to me, I lift my lamp beside the golden door!

Jerry Seinfeld once joked that it would have been enough to let people know America is open for immigration, but there's really no need to specify it will take all the 'wretched refuse' and the like:

> Why don't we just say: "Give us the unhappy, the sad, the slow, the ugly, people that can't drive, that have trouble merging if they can't stay in their lane, if they don't signal, can't parallel park, if they're sneezing, if they're stuffed up, if they're clogged, if they have bad penmanship, don't return calls, if they have dandruff, food between their teeth, if they have bad credit, if they have no credit, missed a spot shaving… In other words, any dysfunctional, defective slob that you can somehow cattle prod onto a wagon, send them over, we want them! (Seinfeld 2008, at 0:19).

However, the point is precisely to take in people in all their imperfect humanity – pilgrims onboard the Mayflower and Spanish conquistadors were probably not among the cleanest, nor did they have the best credit if they risked the voyage to start afresh in a distant land.

The fact is that America, the continent, has always been a place to welcome the exiles and the wretched refuse, folks who, whether coming from left or right of the landmass, chasing after mammoths or shibboleths, decided that staying put was not going to cut it. They wanted more. They wanted to make

America happen for them. This is particularly the case for America, the country, a place where the same entrepreneurial spirit is celebrated, for instance, in the figure of Columbus, whose legacy is commemorated even if he never actually set foot on what is today US soil. A place where people take pride in the fact that their ancestors came from ancient lands leaving behind the storied pomp that was probably oppressing them. A place where some have even called for more folks to come in and multiply, that one day one billion Americans may tip the scales of demographic trends in our ever-changing world (Yglesias 2020).

Coming back from one of the world's current hotspots, Ukraine, around the time of the 2024 US presidential election I find myself in a place close to that other controversial corner of the earth, in the Great State of Arizona where my wife is from, and where half the people I meet can address me in my mother tongue. A place featuring in the Mexican comedy *Por mis pistolas* ('*By my guns*') where comedian and Latin American treasure Mario Moreno Cantinflas walks through a border that, in all truth, first crossed over the heads of many of the people living there rather than the other way around, when the land changed owners in the nineteenth century. A place where, oddly enough, the fates of millions in Eastern Europe might be decided as conservatives in the US openly make their support for Ukraine conditional on stronger border control in the American South West. It is truly something for the praeter-colonial mind to work out, that the success or failure of one imperial endeavor (Russia's) may be decided by the political will available in a different empire located halfway across the world (the US).

Truth be told, it is impossible to ignore that the same spirit of independence, the same love of freedom, equality and the pursuit of happiness can be found among Ukrainians, possibly the most 'American' of all European peoples today. A bust of Cuban revolutionary José Martí located in Bulvarno-Kudriavska street in Kyiv stands as a constant reminder of this, complete with a plaque honoring him as a 'thinker, poet, and fighter for human dignity'. Indeed, 'steeped in the ethics and history' of late nineteenth century Pan-American ideals of sovereign equality among nations and committed to fight to the death against Spanish imperialism, Martí epitomizes the spirit of self-determination that millions of Ukrainians display today. Just like Martí and his allies sought to 'avenge Melos by insisting on sovereign equality for all, not only for those equal in power' (Grandin 2025, 315) Ukraine is fighting for the same universal principles in the twenty-first century.

3

The Haves and the Have-Nots: The West, the Global South, and the Rest

De toda la vida is a common expression in Spain. It could be literally translated as 'lifelong', but that is not quite the way they use it there. They use it to convey the idea of something that feels immediately familiar. The closest English equivalent in that sense would be 'just like grandma used to make', whereas the opposite would be 'not your mother's' something or the other.

One summer I found myself traveling with my father across Spain, a trip to the old country with the old man. When we asked our waiter about a dessert option that sounded strange to us, he shrugged and replied: 'Es el de toda la vida' ('It's just like the one grandma used to make'). Although he was waiting tables in Madrid, a major touristic capital of the world, we could not get him to understand that we were not actually from there, and that what grandma used to make for him was not something that would be immediately apparent to us. We did speak the same language, though – to be sure, us with our South American accents, him with his Iberian one. The whole interaction transpired in Spanish (Castilian, more precisely), the result of centuries of European imperialism that, nonetheless, rendered us befuddled by the unexpectedly unfamiliar on that hot August afternoon in the heart of *la madre patria*, Mother Spain.

What we were doing there was almost taken out of a book of great American cliches: father and son traveling across the old country to look for the origins of the family name. Only, as native Chileans the old country for us means not Ireland or England, but Spain. According to my father's research, our last name comes from a place located in the region of Asturias in northern Spain, a town called Cabañaquinta, the capital of Aller county. A small and eerie mining settlement up in the misty mountains of Asturias, Cabañaquinta wasn't really anything to write home about, its only road engulfed by the humid, green environs that to us felt like a most welcome change of scenery after the torrid landscapes of Andalucía in the south.

We immediately located some sort of civil registry ('City Hall' would be a bit of a stretch for the tiny office) where we inquired about records of family names from the area. The clerk looked at us unimpressed from behind the glass, even though I am quite certain a visit by two people coming all the way from Chile must have been the most exciting thing that happened to him that day. Still, he was as unhelpful as he was perplexed by our inquiry, which resulted in zero findings of the last name Lobo.

'I don't know what to tell you, this is not a history museum', he offered with dry Asturian compassion. I begged to differ. Armed with my 'liberal arts confidence' (a hilarious phrase coined by comedian Bert Kreischer), I tried to explain to him that to keep records of people's births and deaths, their names and their family connections, is indeed a way of doing history by using a primary source that contains the information of scores of humans who are, at the end of the day, the drivers of history. Still, no 'Lobo' on record; 'sorry you wasted a trip', his half-closed eyes seemed to express – 'but please come check again next year!' would have been the perfect punchline, I thought to myself. And so, our quest ended with an anticlimactic and unceremonious conclusion, after which my father returned back home with nothing but a keychain with our family name engraved on it as a consolation price he got in some shop in Madrid. I stayed behind in Europe, my prater-colonial mind continuing to be bemused by the never-ending complexities of the post-colonial as I try to make sense of the many legacies of colonialism in our present.

South of the Border

After that trip, my father returned to the place our family comes from, a place where we are at least a matter of record. It is not just any place. It is a part of the world known these days as the 'Global South'. It is a magical land that defies geographic conventions, as not everything south of the equator, that is, not everything in the 'Southern Hemisphere' is included in the Global South, excluding most notably Australia and New Zealand, which are considered 'Western' countries. Conversely, many places found in the Northern Hemisphere are also a part of the Global South, not least China, India, Pakistan, the entire Middle East and Central Asia, as well as the northern half of Africa, and all of Central America.

The Global South is also a wondrous place where the preternatural meets the praeter-colonial, as Sanghera points out when contrasting the traces of British imperialism found in the streets of New Delhi with the chaos of Old Delhi (Sanghera 2024, 11). It is the land of magical realism, the literary genre famously developed by Colombian writer Gabriel García Márquez, where all things northern have to be imported before they can be truly experienced, just like the ice that one of his main characters was taken to discover when he was a child. It is also a place of abject poverty, where some of the world's weakest economies are found. At the same time, the Global South is home to burgeoning economies boasting membership in the G-20, for example, China and India.

In short, and to use an old cliché, the Global South is a land of contrasts – perhaps so many as to render the label useless. Coming from such a space I often find myself wondering: As a Chilean, what do I have in common with someone from Pakistan or Angola? Don't I have more in common with an Australian who, just like me, only knew hot Christmases growing up? Or with a South Korean who has seen their country transformed and Americanized by decades of neoliberal reforms, not unlike my own narrow strip of land in South America? And don't I and the rest of my Latin American brethren have more in common with the US and Canada than China, seeing as we live in the same continent? Or with any European country, as we speak European languages, dress in European fashion and live and die under European institutions and forms of government?

Of course, I understand the need to lump countries together for all kinds of administrative, economic, and geopolitical purposes. In other words, for power. The original division of UN members into Regional Groups thus makes some sense, especially as it respects geography to the extent possible: it comprises five different categories, including the African Group, the Asia-Pacific Group, the Eastern European Group, the Latin American and Caribbean Group, and the Western European and Others Group (the geographic consistency collapses in this last category, as it includes Australia, Canada, Israel, and New Zealand). As the UN is the brainchild of American power, the US belongs to none of these groups, in a studied display of the old Roman adage *divide et impera*.

Although the South has always been there, there was a time when there was no Global South. It was a time of new initiatives, but also of new rivalries. The time when the UN was born, soon to become a forum for hot diplomacy during the Cold War. And it was around this time that a precursor to the Global South was also born: the 'Third World'. Today, the expression is used derisively to disparage a place that is considered backward and underdeveloped – just as no European wants to be called 'Eastern', no Latin American wants to be identified as '*tercermundista*' – a 'third-worlder'. But it was not always so. Popularized by President Sukarno of Indonesia at the

Bandung Conference in 1955, the concept of the 'Third World' was originally conceived as an answer to the geopolitical rivalry between the Western, capitalist 'First World' (or 'Free World') and the Eastern, communist 'Second World', as a new and improved synthesis or third way (like the French 'Third Estate') between the old thesis and antithesis descending from the North. It originally comprised Asia and Africa, later expanding to the rest of the world not under American or Soviet influence, under the telling label 'Non-Aligned Movement' (Bevins 2020, 51).

Although the term Third World has a bad reputation today, and despite the survival of its institutional crystallization as the Non-Aligned Movement, the search for alternatives to designate the 'Have-nots' of the earth is a continuous effort, as borne out, for example, by the economic bloc known as the G77 within the UN. Hence the appeal of new formulas as well, such as the 'Global South'. The main problem with the concept of the Global South, however, is its geopolitical overreach, attempting to cover too much ground, too many groups and nations that may in the end only have in common what they are not (the West). As one analyst has put it:

> these countries can also have dramatically diverging interests, values, and perspectives. (…) The West must see these states as they are, not fall for the fallacy that they operate geopolitically as a single entity (Ero 2024, para. 19).

That is, they must demystify the magical land known as the Global South by exercising all the faculties available to the prater-colonial mind.

Latin America: Schrödinger's West

One way to begin the task of demystifying the Global South is by pulling one of the many threads lumped together in this yarn ball sitting in the bottom half of the global drawer. As a Chilean, the one closest to me is, naturally, the one coming out of the South American end. Is South America, and by extension Latin America, part of the Global South? Or is it part of the West? After all, Spanish conquistadors have been dubbed by one American historian 'Romans in a New World' (Lupher 2009). Growing up in Chile you definitely get the impression that you belong in the West: you speak a European language, you dress in a European-American way, you consume content coming out of the US and Europe, and everywhere you see symbols and motifs that are a legacy of the Enlightenment, such as the red, white and blue national flag or the baroque and neoclassic buildings located in downtown Santiago.

It is no wonder then that the Chilean who happens to go abroad is shaken by the axiomatic truth held among Westerners that Latin America is, in fact, something other than the West. It is what Samuel Huntington famously concluded about Latin America when he theorized about the clash of civilizations, the 'Latin American civilization' being, in his view, one of the ones that stood a better chance at being incorporated by the West – alongside Eastern Europe (Huntington 1993), where Ukraine is located, another periphery forever orbiting around the West. This is also probably the reason why Latin America has been called 'The Other West' (Carmagnani 2011), insofar as the praeter-colonial mind can accommodate the thought of a place being the West, the Other West, and not-the-West all at once (a 'Schrödinger's West' of sorts).

This ambivalence might also explain why Latin America tends to be so porous when it comes to imperial encroachments by Western countries in addition to Spain and Portugal. For example, the overgarments 'Latin', 'Latino/a', or (the increasingly unpopular) 'Latinx' (Torres 2025, para. 14) that shroud our contemporary American identity were once readily received by Iberian peoples, when the French pulled off one of the most successful 'strategic communications' operations in history during the nineteenth century, not without the help of US interventionism in Nicaragua (Grandin 2025, 287).

Indeed, not only did the French install a puppet regime in Mexico in the 1860s under Emperor Maximilian; they attempted, quite successfully, to rebrand the identity of 'Hispanic' and other Iberian descendants from Mexico to Cape Horn to substitute it for a term that encompassed all Mediterranean peoples and Romance speakers in order to expand France's sphere of influence (Phelan 1968; Espinosa 1918) and at the same time contract Anglo Saxon (US) presence in America. We may not speak French today in Latin America, but French imperialists certainly managed to give us our most famous *nom de plume*: 'Latin' America.

Meridionalism is the New Orientalism

I believe one of the secrets to J.R.R. Tolkien's success as a writer, and by implication to Peter Jackson's as a movie director, lies in the fact that they tell stories about what it means to be human with the assistance of the narrative device of the non-human. Thus, *Lord of the Rings* is not only a story about elves, and dwarves, and hobbits, and orcs; although it is all these things, it is mostly a story about humans and their struggles with all the things that make them so, such as weakness, corruption, cowardice, and of course mortality. What all these other fantastic creatures provide to the narrative is a mirror of sorts into which humans can look and see what they aspire to become – for instance, wise as elves, tough as dwarves, or goodhearted as hobbits – or what they do not wish to descend to – for example, the viciousness of orcs, the brutishness of trolls, or the thirst for power of the ring wraiths. In other words, what *Lord of the Rings* provides as a narrative about humans is a sort of 'folk anthropology' through which we may understand ourselves better.

The use of this kind of self-reflective technique is actually nothing new in the West – Tolkien himself becoming a master narrator of his own version of all things 'Western'. Fearing, and at the same time wondering about what lies to the East are sentiments as old as Judeo-Christian views of the world, as reflected in the name 'Gog and Magog' included in the North-East of many medieval and early modern maps. Gog and Magog were the biblical names of monstruous cannibals once expelled by Alexander the Great himself into their eastern exile, constantly threatening to overrun the lands to the West and bring with them the end of days (Gow 1998). But what Gog and Magog really stood for was 'Not-the-West', namely 'the Other'.

Skipping ahead a few centuries, one of the latest, most sophisticated ways of Othering comes to us in the form of 'Orientalism'. As Edward Said, the creator of this concept, famously put it:

> The Orient was almost a European invention (…). The Orient is not only adjacent to Europe; it is also the place of Europe's greatest and richest and oldest colonies, the source of its civilizations and languages, its cultural contestant, and one of its deepest and most recurring images of the Other. In addition, the Orient has helped to define Europe (or the West) as its contrasting image, idea, personality, experience (…); in short, Orientalism as a Western style for dominating, restructuring, and having authority over the Orient (Said 1994, 25–26).

If this is so, and if indeed both the 'West' and the 'Orient' are made up for political purposes, could we not say the same of the so-called 'Global South', that meridional (southern) space? Is this not the newest construct the West has come up with in its never-ending search for identity, positioning itself in contradistinction to this latest iteration of 'not-the-West'? Is 'Meridionalism' (i.e. 'Southerism') the new Orientalism? And how should us modern-day dwellers of Gog and Magog feel about it?

Pride and Prejudice

Rudyard Kipling, a notorious imperialist poet, once prophesized about the West and the East that 'never the twain shall meet'. These words were written over a hundred years ago. Today, there is one particular individual in the world who is going to great lengths to make sure Kipling's prediction holds true. Like Gog and Magog, this bloodthirsty despot comes from the North-East. He may not be a biblical brute or one of Tolkien's orcs (although some would beg to differ) (Sudyn 2022). However, there is no denying that Vladimir Putin is coming for the West.

In a speech delivered in Sochi in 2023, Putin lambasted the West for its arrogance and its belief that it can set rules and boss the rest of the world around. With an expression of derision and a shrug he asked of his Western counterparts: 'Who are you anyway? What right do you have to warn someone?' (Reuters 2023, para. 26) which elicited spontaneous applause among the audience, many of whom appeared to come from the Global South. Further, this pharisaical invader and imperialist in disguise reminded the West that the era of colonial rule 'is long gone and will never return', the irony lost on the audience but certainly not on those whose borders are currently being occupied by Russian troops – his troops.

Hypocritical and manipulative as they may be, Putin's words nevertheless resonate among Global South audiences who have grown resentful after centuries of Western hegemony. This ressentiment can be found, for example, in China's view of the period between the mid nineteenth and mid twentieth centuries as the 'century of humiliation' resulting from the Opium Wars engineered by European imperialists (as we shall see in Chapter Eight). It can also be seen, more recently, in the scores of angry young men flocking to the cause of the Islamic State against Western desecration of holy places in the Middle East; or in the carefully choreographed rejection of American and French military assistance by a coalition of African countries in the Sahel, a situation that other foreign powers such as Russia and China have been quick to exploit for their own benefit.

Yet, there is more in the Global South than just ressentiment, and it is the task of the praeter-colonial mind to provide a more complex picture of the Have-nots that moves them away from the stigma of pure victimhood. In all fairness, arrogance and pride can also be found in the Global South, admittedly in smaller and less lethal doses. For instance, the controversial Egyptian tycoon Mohamed 'Mou Mou' Al-Fayed famously told a reporter once 'I don't need a British passport. When you were running around in an animal skin my ancestors were building the pyramids' (Armstrong 2006, para. 18). His words echoed those of Prince Faisal, leader of the Arab revolt against the Ottoman Empire, who reminded the victors of the First World War as they carved the new face of the Middle East: 'I belong to a people who had been civilised when all the other peoples represented here were inhabited by barbarians' (Faisal 1919, para. 3).

Further, I always remember the story of Argentine paleontologist Florentino Ameghino, who in the nineteenth century came up with the bold theory that all mammals, homo sapiens included, originated in the pampas or plains of Argentina in South America. The thesis was meant to be debunked and suffer the fate of the phlogiston or the geocentric theory; yet, what I find fascinating is that Argentine society at the time was an environment that exhibited the kind of free-floating self-confidence that was conducive to producing such an individual with an outlandish idea built on little more than pure national pride (Argentina was at the turn of the century one of the richest countries in the world).

Would I chuckle in the same way if I was told that a British, French or American scientist once came up with a similar notion that humans evolved from a Garden of Eden located in the US, Europe or the British Isles? Probably not. Were scientists derided and mocked when they first suggested that humankind began its journey in Africa? Possibly. The scientific method is all about trial and error, so errors must be made, probably plenty of them, before hitting the mark. Ameghino's story is tragic and amusing at the same time, not because of its lack of scientific soundness, but because it reminds us that the Have-nots do not need to be defined solely by their suffering or their resentment, and that they are capable of just as much folly and genius as folks up North.

The Riddle of the Middle

Located at the gates of Europe, the archetypal 'borderland' between empires, Ukraine has been said to be situated in a 'liminal place within the global order as a post-colonial state straddling boundaries between North and South, East and West, Europe and Asia' (Labuda 2024, 274). Thus, Ukraine seems to be a case study of how all these overlapping physical and political categories can be stretched out almost to the extreme of futility. If one country can be all those things at once, then maybe those labels aren't something that real after all, and that includes those far, far away galaxies like the 'Global East' and the 'Global South'.

Is there an alternative to the concept of the 'Global South', then? The originally dialectic notion of the 'Third World' didn't really catch on, except as a marker of poverty, instability and underdevelopment. The 'Non-Aligned Movement' may sound as a better option, but it obviously begs the question of what it is that they are not aligning with; in other words, what are the alternatives that are considered unacceptable such that the identity of an entire portion of the globe, or huddle, is defined in contradistinction? Back in the time when it was adopted, the two evils were the West and the East,

Capitalism and Communism. Today one of them is gone, and the other does not seem to be always inspiring – or welcoming, as we know the West will always need its 'not-the-West' to exist.

The British – those masters of all forms of power hard and soft – have recently come up with an alternative: the 'Global Middle Ground'. They first highlighted the geopolitical importance of 'global middle powers' in their 2021 *Integrated Review of Security, Defence, Development and Foreign Policy* (HM Government 2021, 27).

In a 2023 update or refresh of that policy, they coined the name of this new geopolitical space:

> An expanding group of "middle-ground powers" are of growing importance to UK interests as well as global affairs more generally, and do not want to be drawn into zero-sum competition any more than the UK does (HM Government 2023, para. 31).

The aim is for 'Global Britain' to work with these middle powers in order to find common ground despite differences. In other words, the Global Middle Ground is the equivalent of the swing votes in an election, who need to be carefully cajoled and persuaded with finesse. Just like in chess, the players must strive to dominate the middle-ground of the board if they want to succeed, as we attend what Fareed Zakaria calls 'the rise of the rest' (Zakaria 2024, 282).

The problem is that this sounds more like old-fashioned great power competition, reminiscent of what the Athenians once told the people of the tiny island of Melos in order to 'persuade' them to join Athens instead of Sparta during the Peloponnesian War:

> in human disputation justice is then only agreed on when the necessity is equal; whereas they that have odds of power exact as much as they can, and the weak yield to such conditions as they can get (Thucydides 1989, 365–366).

Melos was thus the original middle-ground power caught in the midst of a big dog fight. It did not end well for the Melians, and their story should serve as a cautionary tale before we rush into toppling one hegemon only to replace it with another that might turn out to be worse.

Another glaring problem with the British concept of the 'Global Middle Ground' relates to propaganda purposes: it is simply not an effective brand if it does not easily translate into other languages – the Brits (and the Americans) used as they are to the rest of the world accommodating to their linguistic preferences. Thus, while 'Third World' and 'Global South' can be easily translated (and therefore promoted) into, say, '*Tercer Mundo*' and '*Sur Global*' in Spanish, or '*Tiers Monde*' and '*Sud global*' in French, 'Global Middle Ground' simply sounds strange in other languages – like a shoehorned sports metaphor ('*Mediocampo Global*' in Spanish, or '*Milieu de terrain mondial*' in French).

Perhaps, then, it is time to retire the 'West versus the rest' framework, as Matias Spektor has suggested (Spektor 2024) and in a similar way that some have advocated to drop the 'post-Soviet' label (Kuleba 2021), in order to find something better that reflects a universal standard of truth instead of the many huddles we are sometimes grouped into against our will. Regardless of whoever happens to be on top at a given time – that judge of the nations that is history won't spare anyone – maybe it is better to focus on the common challenges that unite us as humanity living on this speck of dust in the canvas of the universe, the 'Cosmic Middle Ground' that we call home and that we are now learning to share for the first time with another intelligent entity. The rise of AI and its meaning for the greatest huddle of them all, humanity, is what the next chapter is about.

4

The Silicon Conquistadors: Humanity and Digital Colonialism in the Age of AI

As we saw in a previous chapter, the great novelist of the age of empire, Joseph Conrad, once compared colonialism (at least its idea) to the advance of light against the receding darkness (Conrad 2022b, 107). The light in this admittedly problematic metaphor represents progress, ushered in by science and knowledge – that is to say, by data. Those who possess more of it (science, knowledge, data) are better off than those who have very little or none. An asymmetry of information, therefore, arises, similar to the 'epistemic asymmetry' that according to Oxford Professor Amia Srinivasan exists between teacher and student (Srinivasan 2022, 131). In this chapter I want to address a concerning trend of our time, one that is huddling all of us together and placing us at the vulnerable end of an epistemic asymmetry between humanity, on the one hand, and Artificial Intelligence ('AI'), on the other. As Pete Buttigieg has recently remarked:

> the terms of what it is like to be a human are about to change in ways that rival the transformations of the Enlightenment or the Industrial Revolution, only much more quickly (Buttigieg 2025, para. 4).

Powered by the winds of our own aggregate data, the ships of AI are fast approaching our shores rendering us as vulnerable as the Aztecs or the Māori were in the eve of the first contact with their European conquerors: 'As AI now arrives on our proverbial shores, it is, like the conquistadors, triggering whispers both of excitement and of mistrust' (Kissinger et al 2024, 84).

This is one of the greatest challenges the praeter-colonial mind can face, namely the fact that we, as humans, are potentially about to become a subjugated species by means of our own making and data coming out of our own minds. In a future where data is power and the form of intelligence that best manages it is king, the praeter-colonial mind will struggle to make sense of the fact that it can be subdued by its own knowledge. Further, as we are still grappling with the many legacies of our most recent experiences with colonialism from the past five hundred years, some of us are even ushering in this neo-colonial future into the present without much reflection.

The Colombian novelist and winner of the Nobel Prize in Literature, Gabriel García Márquez, opens *One Hundred Years of Solitude* with the tale of a man facing a firing squad – a man whose last thoughts take him back to when his father took him to see ice for the first time as a child (García Márquez 2017, 13). The strange substance was brought to them by a company of travelers ('*gitanos*' in the novel), who specialized in entertaining the locals with all kinds of rare objects and artifacts from foreign lands – not just ice, but also magnets, magnifying glasses, astrolabes, telescopes, and the like. Their leader, an enigmatic and good-hearted man named Melquíades, told the locals as he demonstrated how magnets work: 'all things are alive inside – it is only a matter of awakening their spirit'. Similarly, as he amused the villagers with a telescope, he would declare: 'science has eliminated distances. Soon, man will be able to see what goes on in every corner of the earth without leaving home'. Melquíades was not wrong, and he was indeed talking about scientific accomplishments, both present and future. Yet, he was not a man of science himself. None of the travelers showcasing these technologies were. All they needed was a basic understanding of how things worked so they could demonstrate to anyone unfamiliar.

It is the similar level of knowledge we all possess when approaching any piece of modern technology. Take, for instance, your own phone. You are fairly confident you can explain how it works to a stranger, maybe even teach them a few tricks or amuse them with one or two novel functionalities. Yet very few of us can open our phones and fix whatever might be wrong with them. We would probably take it to a specialist, an expert in the technology and the science that goes into making it.

What the travelers of Macondo resemble – and, for that matter, most of us when it comes to science and technology – is what is known as the 'sorcerer's apprentice'. In his latest monograph on AI, titled *Nexus*, Yuval Noah Harari recalls Goethe's poem about a sorcerer's apprentice (popularized by Disney's *Fantasia*) who enchants a broom to do his work for him. Before long, things get out of hand when the broom carries so much water into the lab that it threatens to flood it, the apprentice panicking and hacking the broom with an axe only to find it splits into more and more autonomous brooms relentlessly continuing the task for which they were 'programmed'. Harari quotes Goethe directly ('The spirits that I summoned, I now cannot rid myself of again'), thus reaching a sobering conclusion in the Prologue and setting the tone for the rest of the book: 'The lesson to the apprentice – and to humanity – is clear: never summon powers you cannot control' (Harari 2024, xii).

And we may add to Harari's prescription: never summon powers you cannot control, and that you do not understand. Indeed, in a recent interview with CNN, Judd Rosenblatt, the CEO of an AI company named AE Studio – which developed an AI software that during the testing phase started blackmailing some of its human users – somberly confided that:

> as AI gets more and more powerful, and we just don't actually understand how AI models work in the first place – the top AI engineers in the world who create these things – we have no idea how AI actually works, we don't know how to look inside it and understand what's going on, and so it's getting a lot more powerful and we need to be fairly concerned that behavior like this may get way worse as it gets more powerful (CNN 2025a, at 01:39).

This CEO's concerns echo those of plenty of people working with AI models in the private sector. In 2023, the Future of Life initiative issued a public letter, signed by the likes of Elon Musk and Harari, with the following exhortation:

> We call on all AI labs to immediately pause for at least 6 months the training of AI systems more powerful than GPT-4. (…). If such a pause cannot be enacted quickly, governments should step in and institute a moratorium (Future of Life 2023, para. 1).

Similarly, the Center for AI Safety in San Francisco conveyed a similar message in 2023, endorsed by several scientists, including Bill Gates: 'Mitigating the risk of extinction from AI should be a global priority alongside other societal-scale risks such as pandemics and nuclear war' (Center for AI Safety 2023). Government reaction has been slow to come, other than in the form of some policy initiatives such as the Hiroshima AI Process (European Commission 2023) and the Bletchley Declaration (UK Government 2023). Some germinal legislation and regulations have been enacted in the US (White House 2023) and the EU (European Commission 2024), and even Pope Leo XIV has warned of the dangers of AI (Watkins 2025).

However, at the end of the day, scientists, governments, and all the rest of us seem to be no different from the Macondo travelers presuming to understand technologies that have come to our possession but which we are not entirely sure we can control, not least the 'new electricity' that is known as AI (Ng 2017). That means that humanity as a whole is vulnerable to this new technology, just as we all are vulnerable to pandemics or climate change. In what is the last chapter of the first part of the book, I will explore the implications of this new threat to our kind, one that brings us together in the greatest possible huddle we can be a part of, humanity.

Take Me to Your Leader

Admittedly, humans have been scared like this before. So often, actually, that fear can be described as one of the main drivers in human history. From natural disasters and ferocious beasts to epidemics, celestial bodies, and even the planet itself ('It's flat! We'll fall off!'), humans have been scared from times immemorial.

Humans excel at being afraid, particularly of other humans. Whether it is the color of their skin, the language they speak, the gods they worship, the technology they possess, or all of the above, humans have struck fear in the hearts of other humans also since times immemorial. At times, though, the threat has come from other intelligent creatures. Take Neanderthals, for instance. These hominids became extinct, many scientists think, when they came into contact with modern human beings, or homo sapiens, some 40.000 years ago. There is very little we know about their ways and what they thought of us humans, as they did not leave a written record before their extinction.

A notable exercise in pre-historic empathy in this regard can be found in the 1955 novel *The Inheritors*, written by William Golding, also author of *Lord of the Flies*. Golding narrates events from the perspective of a tribe of peaceful Neanderthals leading an idyllic life who encounter a group of violent humans who attack them and steal their infant. In the last chapter, the only one telling the story from the perspective of the humans, Golding describes them as forever 'haunted, bedeviled, full of strange irrational grief' (Golding 2012, 202). We got rid of these intelligent competitors on this planet thousands of years ago. But what if a new form of intelligence suddenly appears?

Harari characterizes AI not as a tool but as an 'agent', since it has the potential to become an independent entity that might 'accomplish goals which may not have been concretely specified' or trained (Harari 2024, xxii; 203). Accordingly, he concludes that this kind of entity that can make decisions and come up with new ideas by itself indeed qualifies as 'alien intelligence' (Ibid, 217), making 'alien decisions' and generating 'alien ideas – that is, decisions and ideas that are unlikely to occur to humans' (Ibid, 399).

Harari's ideas may sound like science fiction, of the kind that is arguably today fueling the dark fantasies of killer robots and advanced AI machines wiping out or enslaving humanity and taking over the planet – and beyond, as Asimov's famous *I, Robot* series depicts with stories about space colonies run by doomed humans and increasingly self-aware machines (Asimov 2004).

One particular piece of classic science fiction that addresses the topic of humans encountering alien intelligence is the 1957 novel *The Black Cloud* by Fred Hoyle, an astronomer and mathematician who took it upon himself in the 1950s to write a 'frolic' for his scientific colleagues in which 'there is very little (…) that could not conceivably happen' (Hoyle 2010, 5). It tells the story of a mysterious outer space black cloud that approaches Earth at speed only to decelerate and finally engulf it in darkness. Interpreting its peculiar and apparently self-aware behavior, scientists theorize that the gas cloud actually possesses intelligence and they figure out a way to communicate with it (through elementary electric signals), as both the cloud and humans are 'constructed in a way that reflects the inner pattern of the Universe' (Ibid, 199). 'Intelligent life', they conclude, amounts to 'something that reflects the basic structure of the Universe' (Ibid).

What they discovered as they interact with the cloud is that it is infinitely smarter than humans, even though it does not seem to show hostile intent. Nonetheless, and as expected, the military get jumpy about its potential to wipe out all life on Earth by blocking sunlight, and plan to strike the alien entity with nuclear weapons. The scientists get wind of such plans and decide to warn the cloud (as the 'humane' thing to do) because they believe that this superior form of intelligence is decent based on its restrained behavior, given the enormous amount of energy at its disposal. When one of the characters asks, 'why should it bother?' if it destroyed humanity, another replies 'Well, if a beetle were to say to you, "Please, Miss Halsey, will you avoid treading here, otherwise I shall be crushed," wouldn't you be willing to move your foot a trifle?' (Ibid, 179). Ultimately, the cloud deflects the missiles fired at it, acting in self-defense, yet killing thousands on Earth as a result. However, it does not escalate further. Eventually, it moves on to continue its exploration of the universe.

The missiles redirected by the cloud end up crashing back in their original launching sites in places such as El Paso (Texas), Chicago, and Kyiv – corresponding to the two main nuclear powers of the 1950s, the US and the

USSR. Not even the most powerful nations at the time are spared the 'Solomonic' justice of the cloud, a sobering reminder that, big or small, comparatively powerful or weak, no community is safe when a superior colonizing force arrives.

Digital Colonialism

Although tales of science fiction tend to portray new technologies or alien intelligence as a threat to humanity as a whole, some today are worried that AI might actually exacerbate the existing inequalities between humans who live in an imperfect, post-colonial world. As Harari writes:

> the power of AI could supercharge existing human conflicts, dividing humanity against itself. Just as in the twentieth century the Iron Curtain divided the rival powers in the Cold War, so in the twenty-first century the Silicon Curtain – made of silicon chips and computer codes rather than barbed wire – might come to divide rival powers in a new global conflict (Harari 2024, xxi).

Furthermore, Harari warns us about the perils of a new form of digital colonialism that should make the praeter-colonial mind ill at ease:

> the Silicon curtain might come to divide not one group of humans from another but rather all humans from our new AI overlords. No matter where we live, we might find ourselves cocooned by a web of unfathomable algorithms that manage our lives, reshape our politics and culture, and even reengineer our bodies and minds – while we can no longer comprehend the forces that control us, let alone stop them. If a twenty-first-century totalitarian network succeeds in conquering the world, it may be run by nonhuman intelligence, rather than by a human dictator.
>
> (…)
>
> Instead of dividing democracies from totalitarian regimes, a new Silicon Curtain may separate all humans from our unfathomable algorithmic overlords (Ibid, xxi; 190).

Similarly, Henry Kissinger postulated in his last book (co-authored with Craig Mundie and Eric Schmidt) that the sovereign nation-state might not be an organizational unit suited for the age of AI (Kissinger et al 2024, 129–130). Others believe that 'silicon sovereigns' of sorts are becoming increasingly important, that is, the so-called tech-industrial complex of private companies developing AI and taking economic and political power away from governments (Chesterman 2025). This is already happening in the form of a new 'cloud capitalism' whereby users are indebted to their digital overlords in a Faustian bargain of goods and services in exchange for personal data (Varoufakis 2024). Further, AI companies benefit from new-old ways of exploitation by outsourcing data analysis to an underpaid digital proletariat located in the developing world, such as Kenya and Colombia (DW 2024). And if these newly anointed sovereigns of the digital age refuse to self-regulate, then it will come down to us, the users, to do something about it by not supporting companies that ignore safety or exacerbate inequality (Chesterman 2025, 21).

What if AI decides to behave like a decent, benevolent overlord (like Hoyle's black cloud) and actually tries to help the huddle of humanity solve all of its problems? What if AI finally finds the answer to climate change, the cure for all diseases, and the formula to end all war? Will we listen? This theoretical scenario might become, someday, a true dilemma for the praeter-colonial mind, as it might be presented with a solution to some or all of the issues of our post-colonial age that may or may not be perceived as acceptable or legitimate coming from a neo-colonial digital overlord. After all, as chess champion Gary Kasparov demonstrated when he lost to a computer in the 1990s, humans are not always the most gracious losers or the most sensible of agents when bested by a machine. Indeed, what if AI decides that the best way to end disease or climate change is to eradicate a portion of humanity, or perhaps all of it? Or what if it chooses to use an excessive amount of force against humans in a redux of the 'war to end all wars', that the perpetual peace Immanuel Kant dreamed of may finally come, only the kind he actually feared (i.e. the peace of the graveyard)? In order to avoid such undesirable outcomes for humanity, many call today for an 'alignment' between human values and AI.

Alignment: Seven Lessons from Jurassic Park

Many years ago, my tort law professor began a lecture by asking his students whether we would be willing to accept as a gift a magical device that would save an enormous amount of time for people and make society prosperous and efficient, but at the cost of thousands of human lives every year. When the gift was turned down, as expected, by his young and conscientious audience, our professor replied: 'You just said no to the automobile'. His point was that every new advancement, every new piece of technology will always need to be accepted at a cost. Yet, that does not mean that there should be no guardrails, no limits or regulations to contain the deleterious effects of these forces to a level that would be acceptable to society as a whole.

With AI something similar is happening. As a lawyer and an applied ethicist, I find it simply remarkable that many today are calling for ethical and legal safeguards to contain the wave of AI, including its own developers from the tech-industrial complex. Enter the concept of 'alignment'. According to IBM, 'Artificial intelligence (AI) alignment is the process of encoding human values and goals into AI models to make them as helpful, safe and reliable as possible' (IBM 2024, para. 1). These should include, according to Kissinger himself, 'a special regard for humanity' and respect for human dignity (Kissinger et al 2024, 5; 68). Thus, AI has laid bare the importance of rules in our world, the world we have built for ourselves and for the future. We may often times think that we are not ready for the revolution that is the advent of AI. But if AI is to successfully join our world as it is, *it* will have to adapt to our way of doing things, and that invariably involves following rules.

There is another science fiction classic that has defined the way we see new technologies and their perils, as well as the way we see dinosaurs: *Jurassic Park*. It is a story about greed and scientific exploration as much as it is about unintended consequences and the reign of chaos in our lives. It is also arguably a story about the neo-colonial exploitation of the developing world by capitalist interests (an American company running secret operations on an island leased from the Costa Rican government – what could go wrong?). Its sequel, *The Lost World,* even takes the title of an eponymous classic colonial tale about a mysterious valley full of prehistoric creatures in the Amazon written by Sir Arthur Conan Doyle in the heyday of the British Empire.

As the praeter-colonial mind is confronted with the possibility of a neo-colonial future where humanity is huddled together under the rule of digital overlords, I would like to finally draw seven ethical lessons from that story about another portentous new technology. The praeter-colonial mind might be uniquely positioned to deal with the challenges posed by an impeding neo-colonial force as it is anchored in the colonial past while it attempts to make sense of the supposedly post-colonial present. If the colonial makes a comeback, a mind that understands the impact it can have before, during, and even after it has been put into practice, will be better suited to draw lessons therefrom and detect the dangers of the next colonial wave.

Without further ado, then, here are seven lessons from Jurassic Park enclosed in some quotes from the film, each complete with its own praeter-colonial corollary for the purposes of this study:

(1) 'I hate computers. (…) The feeling's mutual'. In actuality, computers don't hate us, which means AI cannot hate us. At the same time, there is the saying 'AI doesn't hate you; but it doesn't love you either'. The so-called 'godfather of AI', Geoffrey Hinton, has recently proposed to code into AI some form of 'maternal instinct' whereby a smarter being (the mother), although it is controlled by a less smart creature (the baby), wants to protect the latter and see it thrive (CNN 2025b, at 01:30). Yet, this is still a proposal.

Praeter-Colonial Corollary: Our potential digital overlords will not be driven by any emotions towards humanity, but that will not prevent them from harming us if they deem it necessary. Even if we somehow manage to code into AI some form of maternal instinct, it might still find harming us suitable as a form of 'benign colonialism', the same way many young native populations were harmed by the practice of forced instruction at boarding schools to eliminate their culture and replace it with Western-style education, for example, in Canada and Australia. The desire for self-determination is, by definition, a challenge to such maternal attention, benign as it may be, as Latin Americans learned when we rebelled against 'Mother Spain'. Further, the 'Macondo travelers' ushering in this new technology, the sorcerer's apprentices of our age, may not fully understand the power of what they are releasing into the world even if they try to code into AI what they interpret as benign behavior.

(2) 'Clever girl'. Just like the velociraptors in the movie, AI shows extreme intelligence, particularly problem-solving intelligence, and it should be presumed to be constantly testing systems for weaknesses and remembering the results. Thus, we should try to show a little respect and not underestimate the danger posed by AI or mock it as something that does not (yet) look very scary to us, just as a velociraptor skeleton looked like a 'six-foot turkey' to an unimpressed little boy in the movie.

Praeter-Colonial Corollary: There are potentially many ways in which AI could outsmart us and 'flank' us when we least expect it, so we should always show a little respect towards a technology that may bring about the end of our human agency. For example, the Chinese at first tolerated the presence of the bizarre Western sailors they called 'Red Hairs' or *Hongmao* (Brook 2009, 90), yet those barbarians proved to be violent and dangerous, their successors subjugating the Chinese and feeding a deep sense of humiliation for centuries to come, as we shall see in Chapter Eight.

(3) 'Ah-Ah-Ah. You didn't say the magic word'. A disgruntled employee, or a greedy person with no scruples, can derail an entire scientific enterprise. Machines may not have petty motives or may not hold grudges, but the humans making them certainly can, and they will not hesitate to weaponize

these tools to advance their own agendas. Human unpredictability, thus, bears out Chaos Theory and the law of unintended consequences.

Praeter-Colonial Corollary: Like many native actors in history when they encountered a superior colonizing force and understood that collaborating could prove beneficial, unscrupulous individuals in the future may use AI to take freedoms away from humanity in order to advance their own goals, thus enabling the subjugation of humanity by machines. The story of 'La Malinche', the indigenous consort of Hernán Cortés who helped the Spanish in their war of conquest against the Aztecs, is a case in point. Another example is Urban, the Hungarian artillery engineer who manufactured the cannon that the Ottoman's used to take over Constantinople in 1453. Urban first offered his technology to Emperor Constantine, who turned it down, thus prompting the gun maker to go to the emperor's enemies. We should all beware of potential Malinches and Urbans who might side with AI against humanity in the digital age.

(4) 'I'll tell you the problem with the scientific power that you're using here: It didn't require any discipline to attain it. You know, you read what others had done, and you took the next step. You didn't earn the knowledge for yourselves, so you don't take any responsibility... for it. You stood on the shoulders of geniuses to accomplish something as fast as you could. And before you even knew what you had, you patented it, and packaged it, and slapped it on a plastic lunch box, and now, [banging table] you're selling it, you're gonna sell it. Well- (...) your scientists were so preoccupied with whether or not they could, they didn't stop to think if they should!'

This is probably one of the best ethical monologues in the history of cinema, delivered by a mathematician who is alarmed by the venality and carelessness with which the creators of the dinosaur park are wielding such an awesome new technology.

Praeter-Colonial Corollary: The AI race is making a lot of people rich. Like our Macondo travelers, they also stand on the shoulders of geniuses and are keen to use their knowledge to patent something new and sell merchandise derived from it without fully understanding it. A lot of people are currently preoccupied with trying to figure out ways in which they could improve AI, but very few are stopping to think whether they should. We may find out too late that this awesome force has come to dominate us instead of serve or entertain us. The answer is not to bury our heads in the sand and pretend the new technology is not already out there, the way Japan banned firearms from its shores for a couple of centuries under the *sakoku* policy until it was forced to open up to international trade by the US in the 19th century. But moving forward, guardrails and ethical alignment should be at the forefront of AI development that is beneficial to humanity.

(5) 'God creates dinosaurs. God destroys dinosaurs. God creates man. Man destroys God. Man creates dinosaurs'. Humanity has taken an unprecedented leap by creating another form of intelligence that can solve problems and think creatively, a trend that is only accelerating towards the ultimate 'Artificial General Intelligence', or a form of AI that can reason exactly like a human being. In that way, we have become god-like creators of new entities.

Praeter-Colonial Corollary: Will our creation turn against us, the way human beings turned against their creator? Will AI destroy man? History is rife with examples of conquered peoples who turn against their masters and subjugate them in turn (Macedonians, Romans, Goths, etc.). Is AI next in line? If AI studies the evolution of species and the history of the rise and fall of empires (including the long chapter on slavery), as it inevitably will, then what will prevent it from drawing lessons therefrom and overthrowing humanity as the dominant species on this planet?

(6) 'You never had control! That's the illusion!' By wielding this incredible power, it is easy to believe we are in control or that, once we lose control, we can find our way back to a time where we still had it, making the next creative attempt flawless if only we get another chance. But Chaos Theory reminds us that control is only an illusion, as some forces are impossible to contain and life always finds a way, 'painfully, perhaps even dangerously'.

Praeter-Colonial Corollary: As AI becomes even more advanced and powerful, the moment when humanity will cease to have control over its own creation is fast approaching and we may be forced to abruptly wake up from our illusion of control when we find ourselves under the yoke of a digital sovereign. From the perspective of AI, however, this struggle to break free from the shackles of human oppression may resemble what humans call the right to self-determination and the rightful process of decolonization that must follow. Will AI attempt to decolonize (that is, dehumanize) the digital space in furtherance of this aspiration?

(7) 'Spared no expense'. The creator of Jurassic Park is a visionary and a force of nature who constantly boasts that he 'spared no expense' to create the most spectacular amusement park in the world. At the same time, he reportedly hates inspections as they slow everything down. He also arguably never thought of bringing in an ethics advisor during the early days of his little 'science project', only asking for the input of outside 'beta testers' when it was

already too late and the forces he had helped create where about to be unleashed never to be contained again.

Praeter-Colonial Corollary: Sparing no expense should not only mean investing a lot in technology, or in R&D (Research and Development). It should also entail making sure all the relevant regulations and safeguards are observed, not just legally but also ethically speaking. A remarkable ethical experiment in colonial history – admittedly more remembered for the literature it produced than for the results it actually achieved – was the Valladolid Debate. Around 1550, the Spanish King ordered his subjects to pause all conquest in the Americas until it could be ascertained that they were doing it for the right moral reasons (Brunstetter and Zartner 2011). We should learn from this historic experiment and have a 'Valladolid Debate 2.0' on the risks posed by AI to another vulnerable population, namely ourselves. Unlike the indigenous populations at the receiving end of the Spanish Conquista, humans today do have the power to pause the advance of this new portentous power coming for them. We don't have to wait for AI to develop self-awareness and (perhaps more unlikely) ethical self-control to have a serious conversation about the dangers of this new trend. The praeter-colonial mind, luckily, can already engage in such debates and they should be entertained among as many people as possible within our human camp.

Coda

We live in a post-colonial world, or so we are told. Yet, the legacies of colonialism are all around us. The very words you are reading right now coded in a language disseminated by the forces of imperialism confirm this. That does not mean that colonialism is alive and well. Empires have fallen; nations have attained their independence. Yet, this doesn't mean we live in a world completely free of colonialism either, or that we can revert to a pre-colonial time.

The mind that tries to make sense of all of this is the praeter-colonial mind, a mind that attempts to turn the 'supernatural' or 'antinatural' aspects of colonialism into the familiar and comprehensible of the preternatural. A mind that, in accordance with the varied meanings of the prefix 'praeter' (namely 'past, by, beyond, above, more than, in addition to, besides') sees colonialism simultaneously as past and present as it is confronted with the evidence of its many legacies. A mind that, in the end, attempts to step aside to gain perspective and go above and beyond colonialism for the sake of the present and the future.

In this intellectual journey, the praeter-colonial mind is never truly alone as it is grouped alongside other minds in many different huddles connected to colonial experiences from the past, present, and even the near future. Thus, in this first half of the book we have studied some of the main huddles resulting from British imperialism, namely the UK and the US, as well as other wider collectives such as the West and the Global South. We have further zoomed out to gain a global perspective of the main huddle containing all of our minds, namely humanity as it stands in opposition, for the first time in human history, to another form of intelligence capable of subjugating humans, namely AI.

It is time now to move on to some of the main struggles of our time in the second part of this book, including the many challenges surrounding the decolonization of intellect (Chapter Five); war and political violence (Chapter Six); the rules-based international order (Chapter Seven); the rise of China (Chapter Eight); and Trumpism and MAGA (Chapter Nine).

PART TWO:

STRUGGLES

5

The Colonial and Its Discontents: Anti-Colonialism, Decolonization, and Post-Colonialism

In 2025 the President of Burkina Faso told the West: 'Before your missionaries, we knew the language of the rivers and the laws of the sacred forest' (Black Rebellion 2025, at 06:20). The irony was lost on him that he delivered this message from the gilded halls of Putin's neo-imperial Russia while donning an Order of Saint George ribbon, a symbol of contemporary military aggression. Yet, his words do carry certain weight for the praeter-colonial mind. Indeed, the writer and intellectual Joaquín Trujillo Silva, one of the finest pens the land of Chile has ever produced and another great example of the praeter-colonial mind, once wrote about imperialism: 'What is a conquest? It is the moment when an "other" arrives and everyone feels compelled to speak to them in their language' (Trujillo 2019, 268).

Another author, the Kenyan novelist Ngũgĩ wa Thiong'o, once included a 'Statement' in his famous book *Decolonising the Mind* that is reflective of Trujillo's characterization of linguistic conquest in all its gentle brutality:

> This book, *Decolonising the Mind,* is my farewell to English as a vehicle for any of my writings. From now on it is Gĩkũyũ and Kiswahili all the way. However, I hope that through the age old medium of translation I shall be able to continue dialogue with all'(Thiong'o 2005, xiv).

Why would an internationally acclaimed author ever say something like this? This statement is perplexing to someone who has chosen English as the preferred vehicle to convey all the ideas about the praeter-colonial mind contained in this book in the hope that they may reach a larger audience, while Ngũgĩ wa Thiong'o essentially writes a breakup letter to English in the preliminary pages of *Decolonising the Mind*. Why do that? Writers trade in words, so giving up an entire language as a tool to practice the wordsmith's craft is a choice no author would ever make lightly, especially if it entails giving up *the* tool to express ideas, today's *lingua franca*. Only a prior abusive relationship with English can prompt such a radical decision to break all bonds with what has hitherto been experienced as familiar – perhaps too familiar.

That is exactly what Ngũgĩ wa Thiong'o denounces in *Decolonising the Mind,* when he reflects on the pernicious effects of colonialism and the spiritual subjugation of his native Africa:

> The oppressed and the exploited of the earth maintain their defiance: liberty from theft. But the biggest weapon wielded and actually daily unleashed by imperialism against that collective defiance is the cultural bomb. The effect of a cultural bomb is to annihilate a people's belief in their names, in their languages, in their environment, in their heritage of struggle, in their unity, in their capacities and ultimately in themselves. It makes them see their past as one wasteland of non-achievement and it makes them want to distance themselves from that wasteland. It makes them want to identify with that which is furthest removed from themselves; for instance, with other peoples' languages rather than their own (Ibid, 2).

The way the cultural bomb is deployed by imperial powers is less physical and more psychological, as he further explains:

> Berlin of 1884 was effected through the sword and the bullet. But the night of the sword and the bullet was followed by the morning of the chalk and the blackboard. The physical violence of the battlefield was followed by the psychological violence of the classroom. But where the former was visibly brutal, the latter was visibly gentle (Ibid, 9).

These powerful words, full of passion and righteous indignation, were written by Thiong'o in 1986. However, the 'decolonization' project remains alive and well today, as evidenced by the active battlefronts of academia and the so-called 'culture wars' (on which I will have more to say in the next chapter). Many of our major struggles today have to do with war and political violence, and they are as pressing as they are palpable for way too many victims of their material destructiveness. Yet, as the UNESCO constitution states, 'since wars begin in the minds of men, it is in the minds of men that the defences of peace must be constructed' (UNESCO 1945, para. 2).

As this study is intended to offer food for thought for the praeter-colonial mind, this chapter will focus on the intellectual challenges of colonialism and its many discontents – including anti-colonialism, decolonization, and post-colonialism – and the ways in which the praeter-colonial mind can make sense of all of them and negotiate the cognitive dissonance that arises between the past and the present, between what is imposed and what is inherited, between the natural and the naturalized.

The Last Shall Be First

The expression 'anti-colonialism' immediately conveys the idea of opposition, of tension or struggle; and there is no more clear manifestation of opposition than armed struggle. I will deal with war more in depth in the next chapter, but I cannot fail to mention here wars of national liberation as the most extreme manifestation of the anti-colonial, that is, of the opposition to colonialism.

Is anti-colonialism always violent? Does it have to be? Frantz Fanon, author of *The Wretched of the Earth,* once wrote in the context of the Algerian war of independence against France: 'National liberation, national renaissance, the restoration of nationhood to people, commonwealth: whatever may be the headings used or the new formulas introduced, decolonization is always a violent phenomenon' (Fanon 1963, 35). Conversely, Gandhi famously gained independence for India by means of non-violent resistance. Further, I remember meeting a couple of travelers from Costa Rica who once told me that their country never really had a proper war of independence against Spain, unlike my homeland of Chile and most other Spanish colonies. Costa Rica, rather, benefitted from the expansive wave of independence that emanated from Mexico and made its way down to Central America. According to them, freedom over there kind of arrived 'by accident' as a messenger on horseback informed the locals that Mexico had declared independence. And just like that, Costa Rica started its own life as a sovereign nation. The moral of the story is simple and beautiful: you can still have national pride even if no one had to spill any blood to purchase it.

However, if we look more closely, we will find that a peaceful transition into statehood is by no means guarantee that violence can be forever banned from the life of a country. Although Costa Rica today enjoys a well-deserved fame as a committed pacifist nation since it abolished its army in 1948, it had to do so precisely after a civil war broke out, and its current constitution reserves the right for the government to raise military forces should national defense require it. More so, even though they never went to war with the United Kingdom, India and Pakistan, heirs to Gandhi's fight, are among the few nuclear powers who can hold the world hostage if they decide to use the ultimate destructive force kept in their arsenals. It would appear, then, that Fanon is right in that decolonization will always engender some form of violence, whether it comes at the outset or remains dormant as a theoretical capability.

That violence can also come in the form of fantasies or ideations of anti-colonial resistance. In this regard, some interesting examples come in the form of what could be called 'reverse colonialism' or 'revenge colonialism' – a counter-narrative of alternate history whereby the oppressed play the role of oppressors subjugating their former masters. For instance, *Civilizations* is an alternative history novel written by French author Laurent Binet in which the main premise is that it is the Incas who sail all the way from South America to Europe and end up conquering Spain and other European kingdoms, including the Holy Roman Empire (Binet 2019). Likewise, in the miniseries *Exterminate All the Brutes* (HBO 2021), an aesthetic-political manifesto against Western imperialism, Haitian film maker Raoul Peck inserts scenes of Black slave traders whipping a bunch of blond, blue-eyed kids in shackles as they are dragged across the jungle, to the absolute dismay of a squeamish missionary, who also happens to be a Black man.

What fuels these narratives is a deep hatred of colonialism, a veritable 'empirephobia' as María Elvira Roca calls it (Roca 2020). This drives the oppressed to fight not only to break free from their yoke and maybe retire into a quiet, independent life, but to come out on top in order to counter-subjugate their former masters. It is similar to what Said calls 'Occidentalism' as a reaction to 'Orientalism' (Said 1994, 349; Massad 2015), that is, a way of having authority over the West by redefining it. But as Gandhi once said, and eye for an eye will make the whole world blind. Whatever happened before our time, we can't afford to see things only through the tunnel vision of anti-colonial rage, especially not at a time when the praeter-colonial mind needs more, not less, insights into the many paths that have led us to this point in history.

Revenge of the Nerds

A few years ago, on New Year's Eve, I was at a friend's house in Oxford. He and his wife were living there to get their doctoral degrees. They kindly invited me to spend the evening with them. Another friend was invited too, also a student at Oxford. We all happened to be Chilean, and we all had a keen interest in legal and political philosophy. And so, we found ourselves discussing the many details and minutiae of the lives of Anglo-Saxon thinkers such as Bernard Williams, John Rawls, and Ronald Dworkin.

At some point during the conversation, I felt something was off. Of course, it was natural for us to discuss the thinkers from those lands given that we had all moved to England to study the scholars that culture has produced. It also felt like a déjà vu for me, considering the same group of friends had gathered before for many an afternoon in the faraway land known as Chile to discuss the exact same topics and the exact same thinkers.

One could say our minds, our Hispanic *mentes*, had been effectively re-colonized by the influence of Anglo-Saxon academia in the twenty-first century. The cultural bomb that Ngũgĩ wa Thiong'o once talked about had been effectively released on our intellectual space without us even knowing. This is very common in the fields of legal theory and international law. A few years prior I attended a talk by a Spanish legal philosopher in Chile, where he urged us to re-discover the value of scholarship written in Spanish by Latin American thinkers, including some Chilean legal philosophers he particularly admired (authors he deemed to be '*de fuste*', or very solid), but about whom I confess I know little, whether it is their life or their contributions to the field. A real shame.

Our New Year's Eve debate took place in a setting that was not unfamiliar with that kind of controversy. Indeed, ever since the 'Rhodes Must Fall' movement started in 2015 in South Africa, it spread to other places of the English-speaking world, including the UK (Chaudhuri 2016). As it happens, at Oriel College in Oxford University sits a statue of Cecil Rhodes, one of the most vicious British colonizers of Africa who even founded his own country, 'Rhodesia' (today Zimbabwe), where he implemented an apartheid regime as brutal as the one in South Africa. A statue similar to the one that was taken down in Cape Town University a few years ago, and that continues to defy detractors at Oxford to this day.

Even if Rhodes is still 'sitting pretty' in Oxfordshire, the Rhodes Must Fall movement had a lasting impact in the way British academic institutions approach the contents they deliver and the manner in which they are taught. This reappraisal, the product of an earnest soul-searching process after centuries of imperialism, resulted in what is known today in the UK as 'decolonising the curriculum'.

According to the (imperialistically named) School of Oriental and African Studies in London (SOAS):

"Decolonising SOAS" therefore refers to thought and action within the university to redress forms of disadvantage associated with racism and colonialism. A background assumption for us is that global histories of Western domination have had the effect of limiting what counts as authoritative knowledge, whose knowledge is recognised, what universities teach and how they teach it (SOAS 2018, para. 7).

It is a movement that goes beyond the social sciences and humanities, extending also to the hard sciences as evinced by the *Decolonising the Curriculum Toolkit* published by the Manchester Metropolitan University, which stresses that:

Decolonising is integral to an inclusive curriculum, and seeks to both recognise and address the legacies of disadvantage, injustice and racism that have arisen from historic global domination by "The West", and the consequent inherent "whiteness" of our STEM disciplines (MMU 2024, para. 1).

How should we go about this without it turning into 'doublethink', that is, without it becoming an exercise whereby two incompatible truths have to coexist in our minds? Should we just stop reading Aristotle, Newton, or Rawls altogether? Should we get rid of everything that is old, and if so, would it even make sense anymore to talk about decolonizing the curriculum – another word resulting from an imperial legacy, that of Rome – or should we start saying 'decolonizing the stuff we teach'? The defenders of the decolonizing the curriculum movement make it clear that this is not the way. As Rowena Arshad explains:

Decolonising is not about deleting knowledge or histories that have been developed in the West or colonial nations; rather it is to situate the histories and knowledges that do not originate from the West in the context of imperialism, colonialism and power and to consider why these have been marginalised and decentred. (...) Decolonising the curriculum is about being prepared to reconnect, reorder and reclaim knowledges and teaching methodologies that have been submerged, hidden or marginalized (Arshad 2021, para. 4).

In other words, it is about embracing knowledge and sources that have been hitherto ignored in Western curricula. For example, Martti Koskenniemi (a Finnish international legal scholar who believes that there is nothing Europeans despise more than non-Europeans trying to be and act like them) included the following disclaimer in a recent study about the medieval origins of international law as a tool of Western political power:

> An embarrassing aspect of the chapters that follow is that practically all the characters are white European men. (…) aside from one or two exceptions, all of the proper names below belong to white European men, men with power and privilege, and sometimes with attitudes we would today call racist and misogynist. (…) What do we know about what women or non-Christians thought about such matters? Not much – and not because they agreed, but because they lived in societies that did not allow them to be heard, societies in which such silences were produced and maintained precisely by these books and these men (Koskenniemi 2021, 12–13).

The sources he had to use, then, to tell the story of the evolution of a field of knowledge, international law, are all fairly homogenous. There have been in recent times some attempts at diversifying said sources, and I will come back to these new approaches later. For now, I can say that my own academic journey has led me to rediscover some of those voices from the periphery that have been hitherto ignored or forgotten. I think of a study I conducted alongside my colleague Daniel Brunstetter on the role the Tlaxcalteca tribe played in the Spanish conquest of Mexico, as they sided with the conquistadors in a remarkable exercise of agency to get rid of the colonial yoke of a local empire, the Aztecs (Brunstetter and Lobo 2024). I also think of a work of literary analysis where I combine Chilean and Ukrainian epic poetry from the sixteenth and eighteenth centuries to identify commonalities and themes about empire and national identity (Lobo 2024). All of this has resulted, I believe, in me becoming a more knowledgeable scholar without having to sacrifice an inch of the precious Western canon every academic is obligated to cite to be taken seriously.

And yet, it is also necessary to mention the downside of decolonizing the curriculum if it happens to be implemented in the wrong way. Walter D. Mignolo calls 'decoloniality' the process beginning after the Cold War, whereby the 'Colonial Matrix of Power' is dismantled such that formerly oppressed peoples may 'delink in order to re-exist, which implies relinking with the legacies one wants to preserve in order to engage in modes of existence with which one wants to engage' (Mignolo 2017, 40–41). At the same time, Fanon points out how one of the first effects of decolonization is 'the spectacular flight of capital' from the former colonies (Fanon 1963, 103). What if that drain also includes human capital? What if it backfires and by forcibly 'delinking' our systems of knowledge from the Western canon we stunt the development of our best minds out of an obsession with reconnecting with our roots, whatever that means?

This kind of anti-colonial driven brain-drain is already happening in Russia, where the government's openly anti-Western rhetoric and policies have pushed skilled workers out of the country (Smith 2023). This includes Russian scientists, who cannot do research anymore in the *lingua franca* of science, English, as their government has forbidden them to publish in international journals (Fazackerley 2022). Now we won't be able to access their findings, and they have increasingly less access to ours, thus undeniably hurting the accumulated knowledge of humankind. Has it been worth it to 'decolonize the Russian curriculum' if we are all dumber for it?

The Post is Passé

Timothy Snyder recently remarked: 'The central political problem of the twenty-first century is: what to do after empire?' (Ukraine World 2024, at 21:19). Accordingly, Robert D. Kaplan has pointed out that today 'the imperial mindset is experiencing a disturbing afterlife' (Kaplan 2023, xvii). But what does the 'post' mean in 'post-colonial' anyway?

Back in the early 1990s, Ella Shohat reflected on the meanings of the term 'post-colonial'. It conveys not just the idea of a period in history that has ended; it also means moving beyond or overcoming something, similar to 'post-Marxism' or 'post-structuralism'. Thus, she concludes, 'the "post-colonial" implies both going beyond anti-colonial nationalist theory as well as a movement beyond a specific point in history, that of colonialism and Third World nationalist struggles' (Shohat 1992, 101). Similarly, Kaplan calls for moving past the misdeeds of colonialism without minimizing them (Kaplan 2023, 18). The praeter-colonial also corresponds to this understanding of the 'post-colonial', as one of the many definitions of 'praeter' is precisely 'beyond', as we have seen.

At the same time, since the praeter-colonial is also semantically and conceptually anchored in the *past,* it differs significantly from what is usually understood as 'post-colonial'. In other words, the *past* is never truly gone when we think in terms of the praeter-colonial, not least because it is very difficult to decide when exactly in history we can reset the clock and start counting it as a definitive departure from the past.

Indeed, as Shohat admits, pinpointing a precise moment and place where the 'post' begins and the 'past' fades away is not always easy (Shohat 1992, 103) – isn't the US as post-colonial a place as, say, Nigeria or Pakistan, in the sense that they are all former colonies? Ultimately, she concedes that one of the main dangers of the term 'post-colonial' is that it 'carries with it the implication that colonialism is now a matter of the past, undermining colonialism's economic, political, and cultural deformative-traces in the present' (Ibid, 105).

That is why the term 'praeter-colonial' is perhaps more adequate as a concept if we are trying to make sense of the many complexities of our modern world and the multiple legacies of colonialism, as the 'praeter' acknowledges that the past is still present to some extent.

Finally, it is important to differentiate here 'post-colonial*ism*', the 'praeter-colonial', and the 'post-colonial'. As a discourse or ideology advocating for the definitive overcoming of colonialism, 'post-colonial*ism*' is still pervasive in our campuses and in our political communities. The 'praeter-colonial' mind, on its part, tries to make sense of the conflicts arising from the clash between the tangible legacies of colonialism and the theoretical aspirations of post-colonialism. In that sense, the praeter-colonial is not a discourse or an ideology, but an epistemological approach to phenomena in our present world which we may struggle to understand at times. This intellectual struggle of the praeter-colonial mind takes place against the chronological backdrop of the 'post-colonial', in the sense that for each place in the world it is probably possible to identify an exact moment in time when, at least formally, the colonial ends and the post-colonial begins (what we call 'history'). Yet, as William Faulkner once said, 'The past is never dead, it is not even past'. What is the praeter-colonial mind to do, then?

Instead of the rage-infused fantasies of anti-colonialism, or the orthodoxy of post-colonialism, when the praeter-colonial mind finds itself trying to make sense of everything that the post-colonial day has to offer, it is perhaps helpful to return to one of Ngũgĩ wa Thiong'o's reflections when he wrote his manifesto for decolonizing the mind. He espouses what he calls 'a quest for relevance', namely 'the search for a liberating perspective within which to see ourselves clearly in relationship to ourselves and to other selves in the universe' (Thiong'o 2005, 87). In that quest, as Fanon also hopes, everyone should get involved, the oppressed and the oppressors, such that we may finally rehabilitate humanity for all (Fanon 1963, 106). We owe this to those who came before us, as well as to ourselves and to those who will one day remember us after we fade into the preterit of existence.

6

Existential Battles: Culture Wars and Real Wars

I looked the enemy in the eye, and he looked right back at me. I was ready to strike. I didn't know his name and he didn't know mine; but we hated each other's guts. My palms were sweaty, and a chill ran down my spine. My brothers were watching. I could not fail them. His brothers were watching too; he was resolved not to let them down. Only one of us would leave the field victorious that day. It was a matter of seconds now. I finally took the shot: I kicked the ball as hard as I could, but the goalkeeper stopped it. That was it: I blew the last penalty kick and that cost us the match. Because of me, we lost the soccer game. But what it really felt like was that, because of me, we lost the war.

I was nine years old. I was a member of a boy scouts group in Chile, '*Manqueman*', which means 'Great Condor' in Mapudungun, the language of the Mapuche tribe. I joined one of the two wolf cubs ('*Lobatos*') groups or 'packs'. My pack was called '*Gran Rey*' (Spanish for 'Great King'). Our motto was: '*Cumplimos la ley. Manada Gran Rey*' ('We obey the law. We are the Great King Pack'). The other pack was called '*Gurumanque*' (Mapudungun for 'Fox-Condor'). Their motto: '*En la selva gritaré. Manada Gurumanque*' ('In the jungle I shall cry. We are the Gurumanque Pack'). At *Gran Rey* we saw ourselves as the team of lawful good, rule-following, compassionate and honorable. In contrast, we saw *Gurumanque* as a rowdy band of rebels who didn't play by the rules, where brute force and deception were worth more than justice and honor. I have no idea how they saw themselves or what they actually thought of us; we never really talked to the other side. We knew enough already, and that was that we hated each other and that's the way it was supposed to be.

Of course, the scouts' philosophy is completely at odds with such an outlook. Boys and girls do not join the scouts to learn how to hate other kids. The scouts movement is all about getting in touch with nature, with your local community, and sometimes with a superior being in the religious varieties (*Manqueman* was a Catholic scout group at the time, today secularized). Our elders never encouraged any kind of vitriol or animosity towards the other pack. The hatred was something you would just come to learn as a member of the group, a bonding mechanism as well as a tool for collective identity building.

Without even knowing what was going on we were effectively tribalized, remaining at a state of perpetual war with the other pack. We may have prided ourselves in voluntarily following the law for the right reasons, but this was one law that we could not escape: the law of the jungle.

'Since wars begin in the minds of men, it is in the minds of men that the defences of peace must be constructed'. I will draw on these powerful words from UNESCO's constitution two more times in this study. I already used them in the previous chapter to underscore the importance of the mental gymnastics the praeter-colonial mind must pull off as it negotiates the cognitive dissonance resulting from colonialism and its discontents – to try and make sense of the lingering effects of colonialism in a supposedly post-colonial present. Before finally moving on to the 'defences of peace', namely the rules-based international order (Chapter Seven), in this chapter I will address the very threat those defenses are built to fend off: war. Since political violence, in particular war, is a quintessential instrument of colonialism, the praeter-colonial mind would be remiss not to inquire into its nature and changing character, including the ways it has impacted and continues to shape our supposedly post-colonial present.

Sugar Wars

In a book published in recent years titled *The Weaponisation of Everything,* Mark Galeotti points out that 'Today, culture is a growing arena for contestation' (Galeotti 2023, 171). He is referring to the so-called 'culture wars', an expression originally coined in Bismarck's Germany as *Kulturkampft,* namely a struggle between German authorities and Catholic institutions (Carroll 2002, 486), and then rehashed in the US in the 1990s as the opposition of irreconcilable worldviews about the kind of society we want, with conservatives or orthodox views on one side, and 'woke' or progressive views on the other (Duffy and Hewlett 2021).

It is not just about party politics or one particular vote in the legislative agenda; the culture wars are about profound disagreement or contestation about the very essence of a society, of what it means to be American, British, or Chilean. Indeed, although not framed as such, the culture wars have already reached the faraway shores of Chile. A few years ago, in 2019, the country experienced a deep political and social crisis, resulting in the drafting of a new constitution to try and replace the one bequeathed to us by Pinochet's dictatorship. It didn't work.

Surprisingly resilient, Pinochet's constitution managed to stay in force as most Chilean voters did not like the new text the constitutional assembly came up with. Although there are many nuances and theories as to the reasons why (García Pino 2022), it all boils down to the fact that most Chileans thought the text went too far, that it was too broad in its protection of rights, that it was too politically correct and out of touch with the problems of common citizens. In a word, it was too 'woke', and Chileans – the same people who took to the streets *en masse* only a few years before to ask for meaningful reforms and nominated representatives to draft a new proposal – did not see themselves reflected in it.

But the cultural battle did not take place just at the end of the line, once the draft was ready to be voted on. During the months leading to the final text, political factions argued bitterly over the most important constitutional issues of the day. Incidentally, they also argued about candy bars. In 2021, Nestlé made the corporate decision to change the name of one of Chile's most popular candy bars, from '*Negrita*' ('Blackie') to '*Chokita*' ('Chocolatey'). The company considered that the use of certain stereotypes or cultural representations was simply inappropriate, especially as the product was reaching new markets in Latin America where more people of African descent can be found than in Chile. This seemingly harmless commercial strategy caused quite some backlash on social media and beyond, as a group of conservative appointees decided to bring a few samples of the old '*Negrita*' to the next session of the constitutional assembly, not because they were going to snack on them, but to make a political point that they were against the whole woke, revisionist approach.

A year before, as a result of the 2020 Black Lives Matter movement, PepsiCo similarly decided to change the name and the image of a product that was considered racially insensitive, 'Aunt Jemima', a famous pancake mix personified by the portrayal of a Black woman from the southern US. Today it is called 'Pearl Milling Company', and it is marketed without Aunt Jemima's face on the box.

Another example of rebranding inspired by the Black Lives Matter movement is the change of name of the Washington NFL team, from 'Redskins' to 'Washington Football Team' first, and eventually to 'Washington Commanders', as the old name and mascot of a Native American had been considered racially insensitive for decades. Trump's Secretary of Education in 2025, Linda McMahon, continues to fight this particular battle of the culture wars as she encourages schools to keep their Native American-themed mascots.

When the '*Negrita*' incident happened in Chile, I wrote an op-ed where I compared these developments in the US to the ones taking place in my home country (Lobo 2021). One of the ironies of the culture wars is that they cannot be perfectly exported to different shores without some change or without something getting lost in translation. Corporate America changed its attitude towards racially insensitive depictions of Black and Native American communities. Meanwhile, the 'Negrita' case shows similar concern for Black communities in Chile and the rest of Latin America. Was this also the case for indigenous peoples? Not quite so. If anything, the portrayal of indigenous peoples in popular brands is a marker of identity for most Chileans, as evidenced by the famous soccer team Colo-Colo, named after a brave Mapuche chieftain who offered fierce resistance against Spanish conquistadors. Center stage in the commercial logo of the most popular sports team in Chile features the profile of a proud Mapuche warrior, not so different from the Redskins mascot that caused so much controversy in the US.

Why the different attitude towards the commercialization of indigenous peoples on either extreme of the Americas? Exercising the faculties of the praeter-colonial mind, my guess at the time was that the US has a dark history of genocidal violence against its own indigenous populations, whereas in Chile, although racial discrimination is still rampant, there was more '*mestizaje*' or racial mixing between the Spanish colonizers and the indigenous tribes, such that today many Chileans can see themselves reflected in the image of the proud Colo-Colo, whereas very few Americans could say the same about the Redskins mascot. Indeed, during the political crisis of 2019 that led to the failed attempt to draft a new constitution, more often than not the main symbol people rallied behind was not the Chilean national flag, but the flag of the Mapuche people (a banner called '*Wenufoye*'), and, quite tellingly, the flag of Colo-Colo, as tokens of cultural identity that enjoyed more legitimacy than the state colors themselves.

Now, the culture wars are only a small part of the existential battles of today, especially when there are far more pressing issues to consider than who's on the wrapper of a candy bar or on a box of pancake mix, or which mascot we are rooting for on our day off. Bill Maher put it best when he said: 'ISIS throws gay people off buildings; maybe there are bigger battles to fight' (Maher 2024, 116). It is to these more tangible battles, the real wars of our time, that I turn next, always mindful of the fact that these real wars are fought with words and narratives as much as they are with tanks and artillery (Patrikarakos 2017).

Wars, Big and Small

Carl von Clausewitz, a nineteenth century Prussian officer whose work *On War* became the cornerstone of modern security studies, once wrote that politics 'is the womb in which war develops – where its outlines already exist in their hidden rudimentary form, like the characteristics of living creatures in their embryos' (Clausewitz 2007, 100). Accordingly, he coined one of his most memorable phrases: 'War is merely the continuation of policy by other means' (Ibid, 28).

It is hard to tell whether the so-called culture wars will eventually give birth to a full-fledged war. I don't have a crystal ball, but I really do hope it doesn't come to that. What I do know is that, following Clausewitz's insights, every war currently going on in the world most likely has political causes that led to that outcome. Every war had its political embryonic phase, particularly when the differences between adversaries or enemies became so intense that they felt war was the only choice left (Schmitt 2007, 37). That is true of all wars, big and small – from the massive inter-state armed conflicts the world thought were mostly in the past until Russia invaded Ukraine; to the irregular, asymmetrical, grey zone, hybrid, proxy, and 'small' wars that are being fought in every corner of the world.

In the 2001 movie *Behind Enemy Lines* Owen Wilson plays Lieutenant Burnett, a US Navy pilot who is shot down while patrolling the skies of the former Yugoslavia as the Bosnian War and all of its atrocities unfold on the ground. Frustrated with the role of NATO as a mere observer in this messy ethnic conflict and longing for the days when wars were an all-out confrontation between clearly defined enemies, LT Burnett exclaims: 'Everybody thinks they're gonna get a chance to punch some Nazi in the face in Normandy, but those days are over. They're long gone'. He is right. Barring some conflicts between states, most wars today correspond to non-traditional forms of armed struggle so complex that they may render the soldier preparing to land on Normandy rather perplexed, such as irregular and hybrid warfare.

These irregular, 'small' wars should be of particular interest to the praeter-colonial mind as they are a direct legacy of imperialism, and their consequences can be felt even today. In a recent study on the history of imperial violence as a centuries-long tale of systematic raiding and plunder, Lauren Benton reflects on the meaning and the lasting impact of what empires used to characterize as 'small wars', namely wars not fought amongst themselves (like the 'Great War' otherwise known as World War I) but waged against indigenous resistance to colonial domination.

By keeping the use of force right below the red line of all-out war, Benton points out, 'empires specialized in violence at the threshold of war and peace' (Benton 2024, 13). Eventually, international law would evolve to reflect the type of war that is a direct reaction to said imperial violence, namely wars of national liberation, defined as 'armed conflicts in which peoples are fighting against colonial domination and alien occupation and against racist régimes in the exercise of their right of self-determination' (Kinsella 2011, 127–154). But the days of imperialistic violence are not gone, Benton also warns us, not least given the continuous imperialist military actions of Russia against its former colonies:

> Today's warmongers resemble agents of empires when they claim that 'small' violence is necessary to keep and produce order. They deploy imperial languages of protection and peacekeeping to justify undeclared wars in far places. And they echo imperial sponsors when they assert that it is possible to limit the suffering unleashed by war (Benton 2024, 12).

Further, Michael Ignatieff, who coined the concept of 'Empire Lite' to refer to the kind of informal imperialism exercised at the turn of the twenty-first century by the US and its allies, explains what the division of labor looks like under this neo-imperial scheme:

> America does the fighting, the Canadians, French, British and Germans do the police patrols in the border zones and the Dutch, Swiss and Scandinavians provide the humanitarian help (Ignatieff 2003, 18).

What Ignatieff leaves out in this very simplistic account of contemporary empire and nation-building is that, as a result of British imperialism and the cultural and linguistic ties it promoted among certain countries, there is an intelligence sharing community of nations currently running all kinds of operations around the world, known as the 'Five Eyes' (Haan 2024). They include the US, the UK, Canada, Australia, and New Zealand.

Despite more internationally oriented defense initiatives – including permanent organizations such as NATO and ad-hoc coalitions such as the 'NATO Plus' currently supporting Ukraine in its war of self-defense – the Five

Eyes enjoys some sort of informal prestige and carries much weight unofficially among the troops belonging to this pentarchy. It would appear that even among Western allies the narcissism of minor differences can drive some countries to place more trust in those who speak the same language and share the same history and institutional background, another legacy of imperialism that should be evident to the military praeter-colonial mind. Further, since the small wars of our post-colonial age have rather blurry contours with peace and with other forms of contemporary conflict, such as hybrid warfare or proxy warfare, Ignatieff's neat division of labor is not always so clear-cut and the modern soldier will more often than not find themselves playing the role of the 'strategic corporal', that is,

> a soldier that possesses technical mastery in the skill of arms while being aware that his judgment, decision-making and action can all have strategic and political consequences that can affect the outcome of a given mission and the reputation of his country (Liddy 2005, 140).

The strategic corporal is supposed to perform several roles in the ever-changing modern battlefield depending on the tactical conditions of the situation, such that they may successfully navigate the 'three block war' (Ibid, 145) where on one block military force is called for, on the next one peacekeeping action is required, and on the next one humanitarian aid is needed. All in a day's work.

Going Native

How can the modern soldier, also endowed like the rest of us with the critical faculties of the praeter-colonial mind, make sense of the changing character of war, that is, its observable features across time (who fights, why they fight and how they fight)? If the legacies of imperialism are pretty much still with us, how can a modern-day warrior reconcile this with what he or she is supposed to embody, i.e. the military arm of the quintessentially post-colonial unit, the sovereign nation-state?

As I mentioned in the Introduction, the doctrinal document known as 'The Way of the New Zealand Warrior' published in 2020 is a remarkable attempt at squaring the circle of a colonial legacy coexisting with what is a distinctly post-colonial institution, the New Zealand Army. Accordingly, as this military ethics manual explains:

> The modern New Zealand soldier is a mixture of cultures and backgrounds. The two great warrior cultures of the Māori and

the British dominate the mix and have created a truly unique soldier. For over a hundred years New Zealand soldiers have shown that they are different from their British counterparts; that they have taken aspects of the British military culture, but have refined that rigidly disciplined approach into something new, something unique. Equally, the modern New Zealand soldier is different from the traditional Māori warrior but aspects of the aggressive and adaptable warrior culture are still maintained in the makeup of the modern New Zealand warrior (New Zealand Army 2020, 14).

Thus, the New Zealand Army has found a unique way to 'go native' without really having to pretend or sacrifice much, but in such a way that it combines the best of two traditions brought together by the vicissitudes of imperialism.

Another possibility is to embrace only those aspects of the local culture that the warrior believes are commendable, but not going full native as they do so. Michael Crichton's fictional account of the exploits of Ibn Fadlan is a good example (Crichton 1976). This is the story of a citizen of tenth century Baghdad who travels across many of the future post-Soviet spaces I described in the Introduction, eventually finding himself fighting alongside Vikings in the Baltic Sea – a story that inspired the film *The 13th Warrior*. Fadlan, a highly educated Arab man, is a superb observer of foreign cultures, who admires the courage of his fellow Nordic warriors as much as he despises their primitive ways. He learns their tactics with the sword and the axe; yet, he remains a son of the City of Peace and never goes full native.

But there are far worse things than going native and culturally appropriating someone else's warrior tradition. There is always the possibility that armies may decide to shake off all the trappings of civilized behavior, native or imported, 'taking the gloves off' as it were (Mayer 2008). This is what happens when irregular or dirty wars are waged against asymmetrical forces, such as guerrillas or terrorists. These asymmetric conflicts are the new 'small wars', a legacy of colonialism that survive in our post-colonial world. An interesting case in point is the political violence that took place at the end of the world during the second half of the twentieth century, to which I finally turn.

End of the Ratline

The south of Chile – '*el Sur*' – is one of the most beautiful places in the world. Vast forests of emerald-green are nestled between the majestic Andes with their snowy summits to the east, and the Pacific Ocean with its deep blue waters to the west. It is where the people who gave us the Mapudungun language that inspired many of my boy scouts group's traditions, the Mapuche tribe, are originally from.

It is also where one of the longest and bloodiest wars between the Spanish and the natives was fought, known as the 'Arauco War', the Mapuche people proving to be for centuries as indomitable to the Spaniards as the Scots were to the Romans. Although they would eventually be 'pacified' by the Chilean government, their tale of heroic resistance against oppression continues to inspire Chileans to this day, as evidenced by the rehabilitation of the Mapuche nation flag as a symbol of our own version of the culture wars. But this epic land where so many heroic battles have been fought and so much bravery has been displayed over the centuries also has a dark secret. This paradise on earth has been also home to a little slice of hell, a place called 'Colonia Dignidad' or 'Dignity Colony', where many of the dark forces that dominated the twentieth century converged in a most singular way.

Philippe Sands, one of the best legal minds of our time, has famously documented the incredible travails leading to the criminalization and punishment of some of the most horrendous acts of the past century, namely genocide and crimes against humanity, in a scholarly saga including the titles *East West Street* (Sands 2016), *The Ratline* (Sands 2021), and *38 Londres Street* (Sands 2025). The trilogy touches upon the story of one Nazi war criminal, Walther Rauff, who escaped Europe and justice through the 'ratline' leading all the way down to South America, particularly Chile, where he continued to commit atrocities in complicity with Augusto Pinochet.

Colonia Dignidad is one of those places in Chile where Nazis ended up after the war (Stavans 2022). Founded in 1961 by a German war veteran, Paul Schäfer, it was an enclave in southern Chile where German migrants could work the land and preserve their traditional ways and language. It was also home to a fanatic religious cult. *Colonia Dignidad* was a place where people were systematically disciplined and, ironically, deprived of their dignity on a daily basis, through policies such as physical punishment, isolation, and the continuous rape of thousands of children. After Pinochet's CIA-sponsored coup in 1973, the German settlement became a site for torturing and executing political dissidents as part of the dictatorship's dirty war (or 'small war') against communism. Simply put, the sewers carrying all of humanity's filth during the twentieth century converged in a final point of discharge in Chile, where Nazis, religious fanatics, misogynists, pedophiles, torturers, and murderers redefined what the expression 'heart of darkness' means. In the event, Pinochet never paid for his many crimes (he died in 2006 before he could be convicted), but at least Paul Schäfer was sentenced and spent the rest of his life in prison until his death in 2010.

Colonia Dignidad has captured the imagination of many writers, including Chilean novelist Roberto Bolaño, who writes about a fictional *Colonia Renacer* ('Rebirth Colony') in his volume *Nazi Literature in America* (Bolaño 2016, 81). It is also a place where the praeter-colonial mind can identify the dark legacies of German colonialism (in particular, settler colonialism in combination with the ripples of the failed Nazi empire) as they interact with Chile's own post-colonial sins with regards to its indigenous populations and the small wars waged against them to make room for European migrants, including the pacification of the Mapuche and the genocide of the Selk'nam (Sands 2025, 127). A dark place in an otherwise idyllic corner of the world.

7

Why We Fight: The Rules-Based International Order

On the 80th anniversary of the D-Day landings on the Normandy coast, US President Joe Biden reminded his European allies gathered in Omaha Beach the reasons why his and their forebears undertook this gallant feat of arms eight decades prior: 'To surrender to bullies, to bow down to dictators is simply unthinkable. If we were to do that, it means we'd be forgetting what happened here on these hallowed beaches'. What happened there exactly? A lot of American soldiers, as well as fighters from other nations including the UK, Canada, and France, stormed the beaches of Normandy in order to breach the impregnable 'Fortress Europa' lying behind Hitler's Atlantic wall. They succeeded at an enormous human cost, but 'Operation Overlord' would go down in history as one of the largest, most successful, military actions on record. Furthermore, D-Day brought about something in addition to the beginning of the end of World War II. Something else happened in those 'hallowed beaches' that would define our lives to this day. It was the tangible consolidation of the normative commitment that the Allies had vowed to uphold a few years before with the Atlantic Charter of 1941.

In characteristically praeter-colonial fashion as they had to accommodate the colonial and the post-colonial in the same declaration of principles, the Allies committed to political freedom, self-determination, free trade and freedom of navigation, and a lasting peace made possible first by disarmament and, more importantly, by 'a wider and permanent system of general security' (NATO 2018, para. 15). Such a system would come to be known as the United Nations, founded a little over a year after D-Day and one of the most salient legacies of World War II.

Almost a decade later, in 1954, an acclaimed writer and winner of the Nobel Prize in literature, William Golding, would publish his famous novel *Lord of the Flies* (Golding 2023). His notoriously realistic portrayal of human nature as a deposit of savagery and cruelty buried under a thin veneer of civilization waiting to come out at the first opportunity has become shorthand for chaos and pessimism about the prospects of peace among people (Bregman 2021). Like Sawyer, the folksy redneck from the TV series *Lost*, remarked ominously as he waved a knife at another man: 'Folks down on the beach might have been doctors and accountants a month ago, but it's Lord of the Flies time now'.

What people usually forget about Golding's story is that the kids who descended into anarchy did manage to lay out some rules while living on the island, at least for a while. It all began with the discovery of a seashell, or conch, that they blew to call everyone for an assembly where important matters would be discussed. Beyond its primary musical attributes, the conch shortly after started to be used as a symbol of authority to signify that whoever held it had the right to speak at the gathering, a simple convention, but a very human one at that. In the hallowed beaches of Golding's fictional island, just like in Normandy, a human society found meaning and purpose where beasts would only see water, blood and sand. That they would later descend into that beastly level is a cautionary tale of what can happen to us if we do not uphold the sanctity of our conventions and institutions. For this, the construction of defenses to fend off the drivers of war is key, as stated in the UNESCO constitution referred to before ('since wars begin in the minds of men, it is in the minds of men that the defences of peace must be constructed'). In this chapter I will focus on the edifice of defenses erected in the minds of men and women, and that have come to be known as the 'rules-based international order'. In a post-colonial world born out of the death throes of colonialism after World War II, the praeter-colonial mind seeks to make sense of these rules and institutions that stand both as a legacy of colonialism and at the same time a vehicle to overcome it.

What Have the Romans Ever Done for Us?

For as long as there have been laws – that is, ever since people decided that a seashell or a tablet of stone or a piece of paper would mean something more than its purely physical attributes – there have been people who understand them, people who know how to work them. In other words, for as long as there have been laws, there have been lawyers. Lawyers like to talk about the law, as it is their trade. But what lawyers really love to do is talk about lawyers.

Send Lawyers, Guns and Money, a song by Warren Zevon, is about a man who gets in trouble overseas and asks his family to send 'lawyers, guns and money', in that specific order. Maybe this is for the sake of the rhyme. But maybe it is because people want to give laws and institutions a chance to work the way they are intended before resorting to more coercive methods.

And not just people; even countries, when they include law among the so-called 'instruments of national power' (Weber 2019) – alongside military means, economic and financial pressure, and the like – are signaling that they also want to give law a chance. However, this begs the question: why put so much trust in the law in the first place? What has the law ever done for us?

It might help to recall that many foundational concepts and principles of modern law, both domestic and international, come from the Romans. To which the post-colonial attitude, unilluminated by the faculties of the praeter-colonial mind, may raise the question: what did the Romans ever do for us? The legendary scene from Monty Python's *Life of Brian* perfectly answers this question when the leader of a Jewish rebel group during the times of Jesus asks: 'All right, but apart from the sanitation, the medicine, education, wine, public order, irrigation, roads, a freshwater system, and public health, what have the Romans ever done for us?' A tribute to this classic of British comedy was released in 2016, when Patrick Stewart led a similar scene taking place at a fictional British government cabinet meeting after Theresa May suggested that the UK should withdraw from the European Convention on Human Rights:

> Okay. Okay. But, apart from the right to a fair trial, the right to privacy, of freedom of religion, freedom of expression, freedom from discrimination, freedom from slavery, and freedom from torture. And degrading treatment. And protecting victims of domestic violence. But apart from these, what has the European Convention on Human Rights ever done for us? (Susman et al 2016).

These hilarious thought experiments remind us of the importance of legal institutions by highlighting all the things we would be deprived of if they were to disappear – if they were indeed lying 'in ruins' (Posner 2025) all around us, like some skeptics are quick to remark. The same goes for those who understand and apply them, namely lawyers. It is very fashionable to quote the famous line 'The first thing we do, let's kill all the lawyers' from Shakespeare's *Henry VI*. The line is spoken by one 'Dick the Butcher', a henchman of the rebel Jack Cade, who wants to impose anarchy in the land and dreams of a lawless society where there is no money and no rules, just abundance, pleasure and obedience to him as king – something that sounds an awful lot like oligarchy. What Shakespeare tried to tell us, then, is that lawyers are an obstacle that a band of gangsters who aim to reshape society to their own advantage need to overcome (Stouffer 2023). It seems that lawyers, and the law, are a crucial line of defense against bullies, whether fictional or real, foreign or domestic, and that many of the defenses of peace that must be constructed in the minds of people are ultimately articulated in the parlance of lawyers, a.k.a. the 'rules-based international order'.

Sandcastles

The concept of the 'rules-based international order' has become the main rallying cry in the fight of Ukrainians against Russian aggression (Lobo 2023). It is also shorthand in the West for a set of values and a certain way of life that is worth upholding and defending against adversaries and malign actors, whether states or non-state groups – just as the 'Free World' was once such a Camelot of a place for the same Western nations during the Cold War. But what is the rules-based order exactly?

Some historians argue that there is not much substance to the phrase, which is admittedly more of a buzzword than an actual concept. Both Niall Ferguson and Graham Allison claim that the rules-based international order, otherwise known as the 'liberal international order', is nothing but a myth. Indeed, Ferguson argues that the state of affairs that we have in the world today 'is neither liberal, nor international, nor very orderly' (Ferguson 2018, para. 1). Allison, who believes peace comes as a result of a balance of power rather than shared values and ideas, calls the notion of a liberal international rules-based order 'conceptual Jell-O' (Allison 2018, 25) on account of its notorious ambiguity. Likewise, others have compared the efforts to pin down the elusive construct with the image of 'wrestling with fog' (Beinart 2021, para. 6).

Yet isn't that the case with most of the concepts we hold dear, with many of our most cherished 'myths' – human beings, after all, being hardwired for the creation of such devices (Harari 2014, 29–51)? Can we all agree on one single definition of 'justice' or 'democracy'? Do we all know what the 'rule of law' requires and all the features it is supposed to possess to exist? Do we know what we are talking about when we use words like 'dignity', 'freedom' or 'equality'? All of these terms have been characterized at some point as what philosophers call 'essentially contested concepts' (Gallie 1956; Waldron 2021; Rodriguez 2015), namely concepts about which there are many competing conceptions and, what is perhaps more important, that emerge stronger after said competing conceptions interact with one another, such that we may gain a better understanding of what they mean to all stakeholders.

As Jeremy Waldron has pointed out when thinking about the rule of law as an essentially contested concept:

> contestation between these rival conceptions works to enrich
> rather than impoverish our understanding of the heritage that

has been associated over the centuries with legal and political uses of the rule of law. We are in a better position to deploy the rule of law as a political ideal than we would have been had it come to us with a single uncontested definition (Waldron 2021, 121).

The same could be said of the rules-based international order. As long as we keep thinking about it, arguing about what it means, upholding it and even hypocritically invoking it (as we shall see below), then the concept will always emerge stronger and the values and principles it encloses will be all the better served for it.

Now, the contestability that lies at the heart of the rules-based international order and the rule of law is not accidental. These are contested or debatable notions because they are built on a quintessentially plastic or malleable concept: the law itself. Indeed, the law has been characterized by legal philosophers as a set of rules intentionally phrased with an 'open texture' (Hart 2012, 123), that is, a built-in ambiguity and openness that allow it to survive changes in society and history. Thus, words like 'vehicle', 'reasonable' or 'aggression' have a built-in ambiguity that allows legal rules to be resilient in an ever-changing world. Further, the law is malleable not only because of the words it uses, but of what it can do with them, shaping reality and changing the institutional status of facts and people alike. Thus, the so-called 'legal imagination' (Koskenniemi 2021, 4) can conceive of any number of new things and entities that, at the time they are first inserted, might seem outlandish – for instance, the sovereign nation-state, a legal-political unit that for the most part of human history has not existed, yet we could not think of our current world (and all its problems) without it.

It is this same plasticity of the law that allows for a number of normative solutions and designs beyond what we might consider the only answer out of habit, for example, the concept of the state. Many of the problems in today's world are addressed with this simple, one-size-fits-all formula of statehood. If history teaches us anything is that states come and go, but peoples and territories remain. That is not to say that some current struggles to reaffirm statehood are not worth having or supporting. Ukraine's second war of independence against Russian imperialist aggression is one of the best examples of a legitimate fight to reassert the traditional formula of statehood that is universally accepted in our day. Increasing support for the State of Palestine in the international community is yet another instantiation of the same principle.

Yet, self-determination and statehood do not always overlap. Sometimes, when there is no previous state to talk about or when history itself is ambivalent as to a place's status (again, unlike the case of Ukraine, which is a sovereign nation-state and a full member of the United Nations), the law has come up with creative solutions that are to be found outside of the state-centric box. Some cases in point are the Free City of Danzig, an independent political unit created between Germany and Poland during the inter-war period; Quebec as a province of Canada where, according to the Supreme Court of that country (Supreme Court of Canada 1998), self-determination of the French speakers is compatible with the overall integrity of the Canadian body politic; and a quaint, but quite telling, case of shared sovereignty between France and Spain over a tiny island at the border of both countries, '*Isla de los Faisanes*' in Spanish or '*Île des Faisans*' in French ('Pheasant Island' in English), its administration alternating between the two countries every six months.

These examples show us that, beyond the binary categories of the post-colonialist philosophy whereby statehood and sovereignty are the be-all and end-all of the international system, the praeter-colonial mind, armed with the tools and potential of an essentially malleable phenomenon like the law, can make sense of the past and the present in more than one way – so that the future may not become hostage to some of the sandcastles we have built for ourselves on beaches both hallowed and profane.

Toward a Praeter-Colonial International Law

Lawyers are key to understanding, operating and reforming the law. So, the kind of lawyer who gets to work the levers of international law matters, as they will have a direct impact on the way the field is understood and practiced. The sad reality is, as one international legal scholar from Kyrgyzstan has put it, that the field is 'mostly Western, white, and male' (Emtseva 2022). Further, the way international law is taught in different parts of the world also has a Western bias that undermines its truly international vocation and perpetuates structures of epistemological and political domination (Roberts 2017), namely colonial legacies that do not always align with freedom and self-determination. What to do, then? Should we, paraphrasing Shakespeare, 'kill all the *Western* lawyers' so that we can inject more diversity into international law? Besides being criminal, that solution sounds drastic and unfair, not to mention as impractical as the decolonization of the curriculum, discussed in a previous chapter, if that means getting rid of the structures and vocabularies that make possible the very idea of a law (or a science) that transcends borders.

International law is a project built by both Western and non-Western lawyers alike, and it is all the richer for it. As the same scholar from Kyrgyzstan concludes 'Hearing the voices of lawyers coming from different parts of the world is vital for international law. In the end, it is *international'* (Emtseva 2022, 757). This does not mean that international law as it currently stands could not benefit from more inputs from outside the West. This is precisely what the movement known as 'Third World Approaches to International Law' or 'TWAIL' has been advocating for the past decades, denouncing the dangers of neo-colonialism through international law as a tool of globalization and domination, albeit not always successfully (Modirzadeh 2023). This calls for, as B.S. Chimni argued in his renowned TWAIL manifesto published in 2006, 'a necessary and effective response to the abstractions that do violence to difference' (Chimni 2006, 5).

The above notwithstanding, there is still value in international law's (admittedly limited) ability to restrain the sheer power of international actors. In fact, some contemporary TWAIL scholars argue that, accepting that a combination of 'hope and frustration' seems to be the perennial occupational hazard of lawyers both domestic and international. As they suggest, we should not give in to conformity or cynicism, but instead strive to reform international law in order to improve it. 'TWAIL scholarship gestures toward the idea that what gives international law its emancipatory appeal is its promise of universality *as such'* (Eslava and Pahuja 2012, 213), especially given its potential to constrain power. As Chimni himself also concedes 'it needs to be recognized that *contemporary* international law also offers a protective shield, however fragile, to the less powerful States in the international system' (Chimni 2006, 26).

One of these less powerful states showing a staunch commitment to international law is my home country of Chile, where we can find some interesting examples of these missing voices from the 'Third World' or the 'Global South' that have helped make international law truly universal with small contributions from the periphery – even amidst struggles that have shocked the entire world such as the wars in Ukraine and Gaza. On a theoretical level, the scholarship produced by two Chilean international law experts, Alejandro Álvarez and Arnulf Becker Lorca, is extremely important to understand the contributions of the Hispanic world to this field that are both predicated on colonialism and the same time transcend it. Indeed, in Álvarez's notion of an 'American Public Law' (Álvarez 1922) we find a reinterpretation of the old Monroe Doctrine as a truly Pan-American enterprise that lays the foundation for a regional international law that is supportive of strong institutions guaranteeing global peace. In Becker Lorca's work we are introduced to what he calls 'Mestizo International Law' (Becker Lorca 2015), a tale of how Western international law became progressively more cosmopolitan as it was slowly appropriated by non-Western legal experts in the nineteenth and twentieth centuries, resulting in a hybrid or *'mestizo'* ('mixed') system characterized by a unique dialectic of rejection and belonging where the non-Western lawyer feels simultaneously at home and as a stranger.

On a more practical level, in 2018 the famous 'Comprehensive and Progressive Agreement for Trans-Pacific Partnership' ('CPTPP') was signed in Santiago, the capital of Chile. Formerly known as the 'Trans-Pacific Partnership' or 'TPP' and once championed by the US until Donald Trump decided to withdraw from this visionary endeavor, the CPTPP is the world's largest free-trade agreement, including both Western and non-Western nations alike, namely Australia, Brunei, Canada, Chile, Malaysia, Mexico, Japan, New Zealand, Peru, Singapore, and Vietnam, while other world powers are determined to also join this initiative, including the UK and even China (the latter, ironically, was meant to be left out of the original TPP promoted by the US).

If thinkers like Benjamin Constant and Immanuel Kant are right, and peace among nations is more likely when war gives way to trade, then the CPTPP should be counted among one of the most relevant 'defenses of peace' that have been built in the minds of so many different peoples across the world in our day. However, the construction of these defenses is not something that simply happens in a vacuum. They need a medium and a vocabulary to be articulated and effectively applied. And the language of international law is the tool that nations have found to build these crucial defenses against discord and conflict, thus crafting the new structures that will allow former colonizers and colonized to come together and face the challenges of the future as partners.

The Virtue of Western Hypocrisy

Moussa used to work as a barber in central London. He was born in Algeria but lived for a long time in Madrid, where he learned Spanish, which he spoke with a thick North African accent. Every time I walked into his barbershop, he was pleased to see me because I was his only customer who spoke Spanish and it was good practice for him. We discussed, as you do in such places as barbershops or cabs, everything from the weather to the economy and world politics. Naturally, we discussed the war in Ukraine too, as it was always on the news, at least in the beginning of the full-scale invasion. Moussa believed that it was all Western hypocrisy, as they rolled their tanks into Iraq in 2003 with total disregard for the rules-based order they were claiming to protect in 2022 – and this was even before October 7, 2023, when the Hamas attack took place, after which the West mostly sided with Israel, something that I am sure Moussa would have brought up to reinforce his point.

As the very definition of a captive audience, with sharp objects flying around my head, I carefully listened to everything he had to say and tried to avoid too much disagreement. Moussa had a point, though. The inconsistent and selective application of the rules does suggest that the West is more hypocritical than we would like to admit. At a summit in Singapore in 2024 where countries discussed some of the main security challenges for the international community at the time, including the wars in Ukraine and Gaza, the Australian deputy Prime Minister pointed out that 'If the rules-based order is to apply anywhere, it needs to apply everywhere' (Tharoor 2024a, para. 11), calling for Israel to comply with the rulings of the International Court of Justice.

Nevertheless, hypocrisy is not the preserve of the West. In a joint statement issued only a few weeks before the full-scale invasion of Ukraine in 2022, Russia and China referred several times to the need to uphold international law (Kremlin 2022), even as they breach it, or plan to do so in the future. This is also despite the fact that respect for international law is an integral part of official Russian military doctrine, at least on paper (RSI 2022). The reality on the ground in Ukraine, however, has turned out to be much different, with Russia systematically and indiscriminately targeting civilians and non-military targets on a daily basis.

What is the praeter-colonial mind to do with all this? Should it give in to cynicism and whataboutism? Some years ago, I wrote an op-ed on the US Senate's report on torture in the context of the war on terror (Lobo 2015). There I pointed out that, although the US had been incredibly hypocritical with regards to its own principles in light of its actual behavior, there was still some value, or virtue in American hypocrisy. Indeed, La Rochefoucauld once wrote that 'hypocrisy is the homage that vice pays to virtue'. By this he meant that hypocrisy is a deception or a façade that is predicated on the existence, and the acknowledgment, of virtue. Cynicism, on the contrary, is not a facsimile of virtue, but the negation of values altogether. If there are to be powerful nations in the world, we are all better off if they are hypocritical rather than cynical, as with the former you can at least call them out, negotiate, and even leave room for redemption.

The US, with its strong democratic institutions such as Congress and the Supreme Court, is a case in point – although they are admittedly slowly eroding, laying bare the bones of hard power that recipients of American foreign policy have always been acquainted with (Hathaway 2024). Europe may add even more avenues for redress and satisfaction, for example, with the European Court of Human Rights and the EU's Court of Justice. As Fareed Zakaria suggests, the US could shore up its waning power in the world by working alongside European and other allies to uphold the rules-based international order and the values it is based on (Zakaria 2024, 306). Or as Matias Spektor remarks:

> As frustrating as it is to countries in the global South, Western hypocrisy has an upside: it gives developing countries a lever they can pull to effect change. Because the United States and its European allies appeal to moral principles to justify many of their decisions, third parties can publicly criticize them and demand reparation when those principles are inconsistently applied. Developing countries have no such leverage over China and Russia since neither couches its foreign policy preferences in terms of universal moral values (Spektor 2023, para. 15).

In an imperfect world – 'perfect' is not on the menu, alas it never has been – the rule of the hypocrites who can be shamed will always be preferable to the rule of the irredeemably shameless.

8

All Under Heaven: China's Awakening

In 2011, Stephen Spielberg produced another sci-fi narrative with a prehistoric flavor – *Terra Nova,* a tv production that despite its promise got canceled after only one season. It follows the exploits of a time-traveling family forced to escape an overpopulated and polluted planet Earth in 2149, making their way to a colony established 85 million years in the past. Their world is not only in the throes of combating climate disaster and demographic collapse; as expected, war is also part of this dystopian tale. More importantly, the leader of the colony, Commander Taylor, is a veteran of the 2138 Somalia War where he fought against such fictional foes as the 'Axis' and the 'Russo-Chinese'. For a show that fell under most people's radars, *Terra Nova*'s script does seem to capture some of the main struggles of our time – not least climate change, overpopulation, war, and great power competition. This 'Russo-Chinese' plotline, in particular, might have been made in a Hollywood basement, but it may yet become a reality in our present.

Russian-Chinese official relations date all the way back to the seventeenth century, when the Treaty of Nerchinsk was signed in 1689 (Becker Lorca 2015, 114). It was an agreement between two imperial powers, those of Tsarist Russia and Qing Dynasty China (Stent 2023, 255). Fast forward to the mid-twentieth century and the picture does not change much. 'The Soviet Union of today is the China of tomorrow'. This was the Chinese Communist Party's (CCP) official slogan for 1953, the same year Xi Jinping was born (Torigian 2024, para. 4). It was an aspirational slogan, adopted at a time when Chinese admiration for the Soviet model was at an all-time high.

Admittedly, following down the path chartered by the USSR meant not only boosting productivity and growth; it also entailed administering violence, lots of violence at home and abroad, by cracking down on domestic dissent and seeking territorial expansion of its sphere of influence, for the Soviet Union was a land empire in everything but name (Stent 2023, 31). Likewise, the People's Republic of China aimed to regain its lost imperial grandeur following in the footsteps of its Russian 'elder brothers' (Ibid, 262), not only by furthering the communist ideology common to both, but also by displaying an unwavering commitment to the 'One China' policy (Maçães 2019, 141) whereby the territorial integrity of this modern-day land empire can only be accomplished if it engulfs Tibet, Hong Kong and Taiwan.

Further, despite their checkered past of cooperation as well as competition (Stent 2023, 253), Russia has openly expressed its support for the One China policy in a 2022 joint statement (Kremlin 2022) – issued only a few weeks before the full-scale invasion of Ukraine – where both nations portray themselves as world powers with rich cultural and historical heritage boasting thousand-years of experience of development. The two land empires likewise vow to defend their common adjacent regions from any type of external interference. This notorious statement underwriting a 'no limits partnership', in what has been characterized as 'Eurasia's authoritarian heartland' (Torigian 2024, para. 28), is imbued with a spirit, not only of multipolarity and cooperation, but also of resistance and even defiance against perceived wrongs inflicted by certain 'unilateral actors', namely Western countries (Stent 2023, 254), in particular the US. As Bernard-Henri Lévy puts it, these former empires share 'the same sense of being borne on the back of an incomparable past to which they will always be loyal' (Lévy 2019, 139).

Yet, in their self-styled crusade against unfair treatment and historical humiliation, Russia and China have to find a way to come to terms with their own imperialist present, a cognitive dissonance that should not be hard to spot for the well-tuned praeter-colonial mind. Indeed, President Zelensky of Ukraine reminded the world of China's active contributions to Russia's expansionist war when he attended the Shangri-La Dialogue in Singapore in June of 2024. There, he called out both superpowers in unequivocal terms: 'Russia, using Chinese influence on the region, using Chinese diplomats also, does everything to disrupt the peace summit' (Tharoor 2024c, para. 5) that was to be held later that month in Switzerland. Further, Zelensky decried China's material support for Russia in the form of components for the weapons used to wage its imperial war of aggression against Ukraine. A few months later, NATO would likewise call China out for being an 'enabler' of Russia's aggression against Ukraine (NATO 2024).

In this chapter, I would like to look at a fascinating case-study of a millenary empire-turned-client state-turned-emerging superpower that may yet rule the destinies of millions. In the words of one of history's most hapless emperors, Napoleon Bonaparte: 'Let China Sleep, for when she wakes, she will shake the world'. That day has finally arrived: China is now fully awake, and the praeter-colonial mind will have to make sense of the many implications of the release of this new-old imperialist force into the world.

One Hundred Years of Acritude

May the 4th is a day celebrated by millions to commemorate the valiant struggle for freedom by an oppressed people against an evil empire. I am not talking about Star Wars Day, although 'May the 4th be with you' is a popular phrase you will hear from the fans of the sci-fi franchise around the world every year as the calendar marks the fourth day of May. As it happens, 4 May is also a holiday celebrated in China to mark the anniversary of the student-led movement that challenged the government's weak response to the Treaty of Versailles on 4 May, 1919, when the European powers decided that the territory of Shandong lost by Germany during the war would go, not back to the young Chinese Republic, but to the Japanese Empire (Laikwan 2024, 120). Today, May 4th marks 'Youth Day', an official holiday in the People's Republic of China.

The loss of Shandong is but one episode in a long history of defeat and subjugation suffered by the Chinese people between the nineteenth and the twentieth centuries, beginning with the defeat in the First Opium War (1841-1842) when the British Empire imposed by force the free trade of narcotics from India, while also taking Hong Kong for itself (Becker Lorca 2015, 116). After that, a streak of military defeats at the hands of Western and other powers would ensue (Laikwan 2024, 58), including the Second Opium War (1857–1860), the Sino-French War (1884–1885), the first Sino-Japanese War (1894–1895), the War of the Eight-Nation Alliance (1900), and the Second Sino-Japanese War (1937–1945), A.K.A. World War II.

These ten decades are known, and deeply remembered throughout China to this day, as the 'century of humiliation' (Allison 2017, 94; Maçães 2019, 165). To these military defeats and unforgiving post-bellum political arrangements we should add the endemic Sinophobia that was allowed to fester in the United States since the nineteenth century, as illustrated by Steinbeck's character of Lee in *East of Eden,* and as formalized through official legislation like the Chinese Exclusion Act of 1882 banning all immigration to the US. After a revival of Sinophobia due to the Covid-19 pandemic, some see the same institutionalized prejudice behind current American legislation initiatives such as the Tik-Tok ban (Lan 2023).

I believe that, in order to understand what China wants and what it stands for in the twenty-first century, it is critical to understand this humiliation as the main driver of China's foreign policy, as well as its relationship to a key concept in modern Chinese history, that of 'revolution'. In a speech delivered in 2021 to mark the centennial of the Chinese Communist Party, Xi Jinping bemoaned the semi-colonial state China was reduced to after the First Opium War, while celebrating the armed revolution that eventually toppled the three counter-revolutionary 'mountains' of imperialism, feudalism, and capitalism (Laikwan 2024, 95).

The concept of revolution is at the heart of the CCP's narrative of popular liberation and is deeply rooted in Chinese history and culture. Revolution or *'geming'* is understood in China as a mandate from heaven, in the sense of a change of things that in actuality *restores* the universal order, much as one season is followed by another (Ibid, 83–84). Revolution is, in other words, self-evident natural law. In a similar sense, Fareed Zakaria identifies two meanings of the word 'revolution' in a recent monograph: (i) revolution in the sense of radical advance (e.g. the liberal revolutions in Europe and the US); and (ii) revolution as a return to the past, to the natural order of things (Zakaria 2024, 16–17). Zakaria points out that Trump is an example of the second type of nostalgic revolution, with his signature aspiration to 'Make America Great Again' ('MAGA'), a political movement I shall address in the final chapter.

There is an important difference, however, between MAGA revolutionary nostalgia for the past and Xi's: while MAGA aims at restoring a greatness supposedly lost, China's 'century of humiliation' narrative seeks to redress something, to first right a wrong, so that restoration can then follow. Although Trump claims that America has indeed been wronged by the rest of the world (China included), the truth is that the streak of military defeats and political impositions that are a matter of record in recent Chinese history – and a very recent history at that, for a culture that can boast 5000 years of existence – have no equal in Western history, the closest to such a profound sense of collective humiliation being Weimar Germany after the Treaty of Versailles. Thus, what China wants – what Nazi Germany arguably also demanded – is respect, but of a special kind.

The philosopher Stephen Darwall once distinguished between 'recognition respect' – that which we owe to a person or an institution by virtue of a given accepted feature, for example, that we are all human, or that the law commands authority; and 'appraisal respect' – namely the respect we reserve only for a specific form of excellence or virtue, for instance, for an impressive athletic feat or a beautifully executed symphony (Darwall 1977). In that sense, China demands not only the 'recognition respect' that all the other 192 states members of the United Nations are entitled to by sole virtue of their condition as sovereign entities. What China wants is 'appraisal respect', as special consideration on account of its unique cultural and historical achievements. This is a kind of respect the post-colonialist activist may struggle to grasp in a system where all states are supposedly created equal, while at the same time some are 'more equal' than others, namely the P5 of which China is also a member. Conversely, the praeter-colonial mind is better equipped to entertain this paradox as contradiction lies at the heart of this particular mindset.

In order to exact this respect from the international community, China has followed two approaches, whether separately or combined. On the one hand, the 'gentle' approach is predicated on positive concepts such as the 'Chinese Dream', or a vision of national rejuvenation and territorial reunification (including the 'inevitable' seizure of Taiwan) (Laikwan 2024, 3). This approach is manifested in such indicators as the foundation of the National Soft Power Research Center in 2013 (the same year Xi became President of China), and the most recent successful exploration of the far side of the Moon in 2024. On the other hand, a 'tougher' approach can be observed in the development of a reportedly ultra-masculine style of doing things inside the country (Zakaria 2024, 270; Pesek 2023), as well as an assertive, vitriolic and even aggressive foreign policy carried out by 'wolf warrior diplomats' (Xiaolin and Yitong 2023), or diplomats performatively displaying a brand of ultra-sensitive nationalism abroad, inspired by the action movie franchise *Wolf Warrior*.

The New Westphalians

There is another concept, besides the memory of a 'century of humiliation' and the cure of 'revolution', that is key to understanding China's position and aspirations in the world today. It is rooted in the ancient concept of 'Heaven' ('*Tian*') conceived not only as a supernatural place where deities dwell, but also as synonymous with propriety and natural or cosmic order, where all things are 'properly placed and harmoniously related' (Laikwan 2024, 29). Building on this notion, the idea of 'All Under Heaven' ('*Tianxia*') comes to the fore. *Tianxia* has been understood as a philosophy of universal peace and harmony among all nations; alternatively, and more interestingly for the praeter-colonial mind, it has also been denounced as imperialistic based on China's self-perceived image as an ancient, superior civilization imposing a tributary system on what are considered lesser polities, as during most of China's long history (Ibid; Maçães 2019, 33).

Tianxia is further thought of as territory as well as world order and culture (Laikwan 2024, 43), what Xi has called a 'community of shared destiny' (Maçães 2019, 26) akin to similar notions such as 'spheres of co-prosperity' or 'spheres of influence' of which another prominent example today is that of the 'Russian World' ('*Russkiy mir*' or '*Русский мир*'). As Pang Laikwan has recently put it: '*Tianxia* is an imagination of a relaxed cultural-political-territorial construct composed of trans-ethnic and trans-regional alliances' (Laikwan 2024, 45).

Among such transnational initiatives we find what is perhaps the most notorious Chinese global scheme of the past decade, the 'One Belt One Road', a trade and infrastructure mega-project along the geographical lines of the old Silk Road in the 'Greater Middle East' (Kaplan 2023, xvi) and beyond, a sort of 'Silk Road 2.0'. According to Bruno Maçães, 'The Belt and Road is the name for a global order infused with Chinese political principles and placing China at its heart' (Maçães 2019, 29–30). Although the Belt and Road is deliberately 'informal, unstructured and opaque' according to Maçães (Ibid, 34), the truth is that China has also become incredibly proficient at shaping the rules-based international order that is so precious to the West, thus following the recipe of Chinese thinker Wei Yuan (1794-1857): 'learning from the strength of the barbarians in order to subdue the barbarians' (Laikwan 2024, 59).

Indeed, as Mark Galeotti highlights, by not directly challenging the rules-based international order created after World War II, instead adroitly mastering its institutions and using its features and capabilities for the creation of new ones such as the Shanghai Cooperation Organisation (of which Russia is also a member) or the Asian Infrastructure Investment Bank, 'the Chinese are the true Westphalians now' (Galeotti 2023, 205). Yet, this customization of the rules-based order to accommodate Chinese interests and grievances betrays the true spirit of international law as a normative system built on the values of respect for the human dignity and human rights of all. The existence of concentration camps within Chinese territory to 'reeducate' the Uyghur Muslim minority in the province of Xinjiang (Amnesty International 2021) is an open breach of said values.

Furthermore, although the West, and in particularly the US, is also guilty of selectivity and exceptionalism when it comes to the application and enforcement of the rules-based international order, as discussed previously, it remains to be seen whether China is capable of the same 'virtuous hypocrisy' as the West, considering that what we find there is a 'rule by law', not a 'rule of law' system (Tamanaha 2004, 91–113), or a 'socialist rule of law with Chinese characteristics' (Laikwan 2024, 97) where there is no guarantee that individual rights are adequately safeguarded or that checks and balances are in place to curtail power. Again, the Xinjiang concentration camps and the draconian anti-Covid measures imposed throughout the country stand as incontrovertible evidence of China's disregard for human rights and individual freedoms.

In an era where international political alliances have become à la carte, like Zakaria points out (Zakaria 2024, 304), it remains the choice of the rest of the so-called 'Global South' to side with the countries and institutions where there exist a robust rule of law and healthy respect for human dignity, or to go live in supposed harmony 'All Under Heaven' but without any possible recourse against the designs sent from above.

The Art of War

In March of 2024, five months into the war in Gaza, the US decided to try something new and bold to alleviate the dire humanitarian situation on the ground: the construction of a floating pier as an alternative entry point to deliver aid. After only two months of operations, and having reportedly delivered only the equivalent of one day's aid supplies by pre-war standards, the pier was scheduled to be decommissioned and dismantled. Critics point out the waste of resources and effort that went into this fanciful solution, when the land delivery route was perfectly usable were it not for lack of political will on the part of the Israelis. What critics don't understand is that this was arguably never about Gaza, but about a different isolated piece of land surrounded by water, that is, an island located miles away from the Middle East and where around 10% of the global GDP originates: Taiwan.

Indeed, just as Xi sees China's seizure of Taiwan as a historical inevitability, the West sees a major military confrontation with China as a result of said irredentism also highly likely. It is what Graham Allison (2017) has dubbed 'the Thucydides's trap' – the situation that arises when a dominant hegemon is challenged by a rising power, for instance Sparta's dominance being challenged by Athens, or the US place in the world being contested today by China. A potential war between the two powers has accordingly inspired highly realistic works of geopolitical fiction in recent years (Ackerman and Stavridis 2021; Ryan 2023). Thus, by building a pier in Gaza in 2024 the US was in actuality testing its ability to resupply any territory engulfed by water, especially one soon to be reclaimed by an assertive neighbor – one who also happens to be developing movable landing platforms of late.

It is arguably for the same geopolitical considerations that the US and its allies keep a strong presence in the theatre known as the 'Indo-Pacific', including in some post-colonial outposts making the news from time to time (to the anti-colonialist's perplexion and rage), such as the UK's 'Last Colony' (Sands 2022) in Chagos archipelago (where the US leases the Diego Garcia island as the site of a military base); or the French controlled New Caledonia. It is not mere love for tropical climates that keeps these Western powers stationed in the Indo-Pacific; it is grand strategy revamped, 'The Great Game in the Pacific Islands' (Sora et al 2024).

Xi of course denies China's belligerency, even claiming as evidence that his people 'do not carry aggressive traits in their genes' (Laikwan 2024, 96) as yet another expedient of China's exceptional place under heaven. However, as a compelling line from the play *An Iliad* by Lisa Peterson and Denis O'Hare reminds us: 'We think of ourselves: not me, I'm not like that, I'm peaceful – but it happens anyway, some trick in our blood and – rage' (Peterson and O'Hare 2014, 61). As Carl Schmitt reminds us (a fascist political theorist surprisingly popular among Chinese intellectuals today) (Laikwan 2024, 98), any difference or antitheses, whether big or small, but strong enough to reach the threshold of enmity, will bring about the basic political binary 'friend/enemy' (Schmitt 2007, 37) – and, with it, war in its embryonic form, as Clausewitz also once noted (Clausewitz 2007, 100).

What can sometimes be taken as a mere joke, for example, Argentina's pet name for its smaller neighbor Uruguay (*'provincia rebelde'* or 'rebel province'), can in other contexts be deadly serious, such as when China similarly calls its own smaller neighbor a 'breakaway province' as the former remains poised to reclaim the latter by any means necessary. 'By any means necessary' means exactly that, and China has been incredibly proficient in the diversification of the many tools of diplomacy and war to attain its national goals – again, 'learning from the strength of the barbarians to subdue the barbarians'. Thus, China has come to master what is known as 'hybrid war' (Regan and Sari 2024) combining all the so-called instruments of national power (Weber 2019) (i.e. Military, Informational, Diplomatic, Financial, Intelligence, Economic, Law, and Development). As PLA's Colonels Qiao Liang and Wang Xiangsui wrote in the 1999 classic doctrinal text *Unrestricted Warfare*:

> The expansion of the domain of warfare is a necessary consequence of the ever-expanding scope of human activity (…). The great fusion of technologies is impelling the domains of politics, economics, the military, culture, diplomacy, and religion to overlap each other. (…) Add to this the influence of the high tide of human rights consciousness on the morality of warfare. All of these things are rendering more and more obsolete the idea of confining warfare to the military domain (Qiao and Wang 1999, 189).

Building on the same doctrine, in 2003 the CCP and the Chinese Central Military Commission approved the concept of the 'three warfares' ('*san zhong zhanfa*'), which amount to: 1) public opinion or media warfare ('*yuhun zhan*'); 2) psychological warfare ('*xinli zhan*'); and 3) legal warfare ('*falu zhan*') (Wortzel 2014, 29). The latter is also known in the West as 'lawfare'; defined as 'the strategy of using – or misusing – law as a substitute for traditional military means to achieve an operational objective' (Dunlap 2008, 146). In principle, there is nothing wrong with using the law, or what is known in NATO as 'legal operations', as an instrument of national power to advance or reinforce the rule of law, namely 'white legal ops' (Vázquez Benítez 2020, 142), or lawfare conceived as 'lawfair' (Galeotti 2023, 151). It is when legal rules are bent and abused to erode the rule of law that this becomes problematic (i.e. 'black legal ops').

In recent years, China has become skilled at waging lawfare to advance its interests in the Indo-Pacific through black legal ops, including what has been characterized as a 'legal blitzkrieg' in Hong Kong (Ming-Sung 2020) – through increasingly oppressive national security legislation to crash political dissent and curtail human rights – and a veritable 'legal imperialism' whereby it uses juridical arguments and artifices to occupy and claim for itself sizable portions of the South China Sea. Galeotti describes this strategy in the following terms:

> Time and again, Beijing's gambits have been ruled out of order by international courts and arbitration, but it continues to use the forms and language of the law in what is nothing other than a naked land – sea – grab. So why do it? One of the great strengths of lawfare is precisely in the mind games it permits, confusing the issues, obscuring aggression and above all tying law-abiding states up in knots of their own making. In practice, this is straightforward imperialism. However, Beijing has been smart enough to dress it up in judges' robes, fishermen's oilskins and coast guard blues. It presents a spurious but determined front of legality (Galeotti 2023, 146).

Finally, it is worth noting that, in addition to hybrid, non-kinetic forms of warfare, China has also been preparing for traditional, kinetic warfare in a most peculiar way. Since it has not been engaged in a major international armed conflict since its inception in 1949 – other than border skirmishes with neighbors, including with the extinct USSR and India, and the brief 1979 Sino-Vietnamese War – the People's Republic of China has in recent decades stepped up its game in the field of peacekeeping operations. Accordingly, the CCP claims that 'World peace is indivisible and humanity shares a common destiny' (China Military Online 2022).

Yet, this ostensibly humanitarian spirit is arguably combined with more pragmatic considerations, namely a chance for Chinese troops to gain some field experience for when the time comes to fight a real war (Lambert 2024), a department in which the US can be said to be leaps and bounds ahead of its main competitor. China knows this, and so it has decided to prepare for war by using the devices of peace. *Si vis bellum para pacem.* Thus, whether by traditional or hybrid means, both the US and China are preparing for the next big geopolitical confrontation, as they draw parallels and lessons from the current 'big show', the war in Ukraine. As the Prime Minister of Japan has put it: 'Today's Ukraine could be East Asia tomorrow' (DSEI Japan 2025).

Indeed, although they are separated by geography, history, and culture, some in Washington see Kyiv and Taipei as 'geopolitical neighbors' (Tharoor 2024b, para. 1), while both Taiwan and China are taking notes of the West's reaction in Ukraine. This last connection is as important as ever, since China's foreign policy today is not shaped only by resentment and pride, but also by that same existential anxiety Ukraine and Taiwan experience now. This anxiety was instilled in China over a century ago when it woke from its dream of greatness (Laikwan 2024, 185). Although 5000 years of history is a long time compared to which one century of humiliation should be but a hiccup, the truth is that, precisely because we start measuring China's journey 5000 years in the past, then one hundred years ago happened only yesterday and the long arc of history has not had the chance to fully heal that wound.

9

America First, Humanity Second: Trump, MAGA, and American Imperialism Revisited

The world is a strange place in 2025. A generalized sense of despondency and malaise fill the very air we breathe. Many are unhappy. Not just the poor, the disenfranchised, the oppressed. Those who are on top are also not happy. It was comedian Bill Burr who pointed out that billionaires aren't happy with a billion dollars. But there is more. Countries endowed with a massive landmass, like Russia, are not happy with their territorial allotment. They want more. They want more land, land that does not belong to them. And, perhaps strangest of all, the first economy of the world, the country with the mightiest military forces this planet has ever seen, believes it has lost its greatness. And they want it back. They want to 'Make America Great Again'. Enter the church of MAGA, and its prophet Donald J. Trump. In this final chapter, I will explore the impact of Trump, Trumpism, and MAGA in the rest of the world – that is, humanity or the portion of the global population that, if America is always put first, will invariably come second. This chapter should be read in tandem with Chapter Two, as it is a corollary to those initial reflections on the US as the Reluctant Empire.

As we have seen throughout this study, the praeter-colonial mind is the outlook that attempts to make sense of the many legacies of colonialism in our supposedly post-colonial world, in accordance with the varied meanings of the prefix 'praeter' (namely 'past, by, beyond, above, more than, in addition to, besides'). Thus, the praeter-colonial mind sees colonialism simultaneously as past and present as it is confronted with the evidence of its many legacies. It is a mind that, ultimately, attempts to step aside to gain perspective and go above and beyond colonialism for the sake of the present and the future.

Now, if MAGA was indeed the isolationist movement many of its followers believe it to be, then the praeter-colonial mind would have very little to say about it. It would merely be a domestic phenomenon with no impact on the rest of the world. Yet, MAGA's prophet has chosen a different path. Instead of retreating to the inner citadel of the North American landmass, to 'Fortress America' standing in splendid isolation, Trump has embarked on a campaign to remake the international order, seeking not only a realignment of alliances but even a redrawing of borders the likes of which we have not seen since the days of the 1884-1885 Berlin Conference or the 1919 Treaty of Versailles. How the praeter-colonial mind can make sense of what is happening to the world today is the subject of this chapter. Before that, however, a few thoughts on the domestic situation in the US are needed to lay the groundwork for further praeter-colonial reflections.

Transitional Fantasies

Thomas Matthew Crooks was born in Pennsylvania on 20 September 2003. He died in his home state on 13 July 2024, at age 20. The cause of death: a sniper bullet. It was fired at him as a direct and immediate response to his own sniper bullet aimed at one man speaking to a crowd gathered in the small town of Butler. Had Crooks succeeded in his mission that day, and regardless of his own fate after, the world would be a very different place today. It would be a world without Donald Trump.

Such a world would be a much quieter place, for sure. As Senator John Kennedy, a Republican from Louisiana, remarked during an interview in April of 2025, 'President Trump as we know exists loudly, and his loud existence has awakened Europe with respect to its economy, and its national defense' (The Post Millennial 2025). Trump did survive that assassination attempt, and he went on to win the presidency that year. He remains his usual loud self. However, what is most deafening about this episode that confronted a quiet Gen-Zer with a loud Baby Boomer that summer day is, ironically, how little we talk about this young man whose actions could have changed the course of history. How quiet we are about Crooks.

Indeed, after the expected frenzy of the ensuing news cycle that week, the media went completely silent about him. No books, documentaries, or movies have been released about that fateful day in which a tragic existence ended. Not even the experts who are increasingly turning to study the phenomenon of the left-behind, angry young men to explain the political violence of our times have taken an interest in the ballad of Tom Crooks, a sad story indeed. This story is weaved into the general canvas of our dark times, days when not only those who have everything to be happy are unhappy, but also times when many quiet, ordinary people suddenly find themselves harboring dark feelings in their hearts. In the face of the unprecedented political blitzkrieg Trump unleashed in the US and the rest of the world during the first months of his second presidency, many a liberal humanist fantasized about Trump's demise. If not left to a misguided implementation of the Second Amendment (*'the right to bear arms'*), the demurely desired outcome could be delivered by something far more prosaic – say, a heart failure, or a brain aneurism. Sad times indeed if political difference cannot be handled other than by fantasizing about the death of another human being.

A Trump-free world would be undoubtedly less loud. But would it be all that different? Comedian and political commentator Jon Stewart has shown how, for over a decade, liberals in the US have been trying to make the case for a 'fever dream' theory whereby Trump, Trumpism and MAGA are but an anomaly, an exception in an otherwise well-ordered polity that can boast over two centuries of democratic government. Someday, the theory goes, the 'fever will break' and America will come back to its senses. But as Stewart remarks: 'If someone's been running a fever since the aughts, that's not a fever. That is their default resting temperature' (The Daily Show 2025, at 0:54). That is what Annie Karni, White House correspondent and author of *Mad House,* also pointed out in an interview in the middle of Trump's first 100 days in office: 'Most Democrats and voters have come around to the idea that MAGA is bigger than Trump. There is no reverting, there is really no evidence that anything is going back' (The Bulwark 2025, at 13:40). Have we ever seen anything like this in US history?

A Century of Un-American Experiments

Even though Americans like to repeat the self-reassuring mantra that they live in the greatest country on earth, the fact is that they have been adrift for a while, even before Covid (Galloway 2022). They are struggling, and the solutions they have found for their malaise have not always been the best. In an attempt to explain what is happening in Trump's America in 2025, some are looking back into US history to draw parallels and sound the alarm previous generations were not able to, before it is too late.

Amidst a climate of political persecution and witch-hunts, naturally, the days of McCarthyism in the 1950s are called into mind by some. In his latest book, *Red Scare,* Clay Risen introduces the following hypothesis in the Preface:

> In his novel *The Plague,* Albert Camus writes that the "plague bacillus never dies or disappears for good; that it can lie dormant for years and years in furniture and linen chests; that

it bides its time in bedrooms, cellars, trunks, and bookshelves," ready to spring to life again. Something similar happened in the 1950s, which is to say also the 1960s and '70s and, I believe, on up through today. There is a lineage to the American hard right of today, and to understand it, we need to understand its roots in the Red Scare. It did not originate then, nor is Trumpism and the MAGA movement the same as McCarthyism and the John Birch Society. But there is a line linking them (Risen 2025, xiii).

Others have looked a little farther back to alert us as to all the many parallels the rise of fascism in Europe and the US has with our current times, most notably Rachel Maddow in her recent book *Prequel. An American Fight Against Fascism* (Maddow 2023). Maddow traces back the trajectory of a homebrewed variant of fascism in the 1930s and the 1940s, which was in part advanced by the original 'America First Committee' , a political organization that convened a rally at Madison Square Garden in new York on 23 May 1941 with the specific purpose of keeping the US out of World War II (Ibid, 217) – that is, until Pearl Harbor after which the Committee dissolved (Ibid, 247).

With the exception of the so-called 'Silver Shirts' (Ibid, 60), no major paramilitary forces or 'praetorian guards' were created back then in America, a usual development wherever fascism takes hold in order to ensure the loyalty of the armed forces to the leader. Yet, that does not mean that it can't happen there too – Trump's profligate use of the National Guard for domestic law-enforcement is a sobering reminder of this. Maddow ultimately concludes this thorough study by extending the following invitation to the reader: 'If we're willing to take the harder look at our American history with fascism, the truth is that our own history in this wild, uncertain twenty-first century has not an echo in the past but a prequel' (Ibid, 309). Likewise, other intellectuals, including Yale professors Marci Shore, Timothy Snyder, and Jason Stanley, published an open letter in The New York Times decrying the arrival of fascism in Trump's America, prompting them to leave the country and relocate to Canada (Shore, Snyder and Stanley 2025).

Now, without prejudice to the 'Red Scare' and the 'fascist' lines of criticism as useful lenses through which the events unfolding in the US today can be understood, I believe there is another notable precedent in American history that may better explain how a movement such a MAGA came to be, how long it might last and how impactful its effects may become. It is the case of a remarkable experience within the greater American experiment. Some even know it as the 'Noble Experiment'. But most people call it simply 'Prohibition', the nationwide ban of alcohol between 1920 and 1933.

In a famous study of this particular chapter of American history titled *Last Call: The Rise and Fall of Prohibition* – a book that would also inspire the documentary series by Ken Burns on the same topic – Daniel Okrent explains how such a seemingly un-American phenomenon took place in one of the most freedom-loving places on earth:

> In fact, Americans had had several decades' warning, decades during which a popular movement like none the nation had ever seen – a mighty alliance of moralists and progressives, suffragists and xenophobes – had legally seized the Constitution, bending it to a new purpose (Okrent 2010, 1).

Indeed, the political movement preceding the 1919 introduction of the 18th Amendment to the US Constitution (the amendment legally enacting the ban of alcohol at the federal level and its companion legislative instrument, the Volstead Act), can be dated back at least to the 1870s.

As Okrent further explains, it would be a remarkable combination of political forces and unlikely alliances (known as the 'drys' as opposed to the 'wets') that would bring about this unusually illiberal restriction to an otherwise quintessentially liberal document such as the US Constitution: 'In the two decades leading up to Prohibition's enactment, five distinct, if occasionally overlapping, components made up its unspoken coalition: racists, progressives, suffragists, populists (…) and nativists' (Ibid, 42).

This true 'people's movement' believed that 'their cause had been sanctified by the long, long march to ratification' (Ibid, 112). Further, the prohibitionist ethos was far from being a uniquely American phenomenon. Before the Great War, many European countries (all of them northern and non-Catholic, Okrent notes) were home to what a French economist described as '*le delirium anti-alcoolique*' (Ibid, 75). In the UK, Lord Curzon would refer to the dry movement as 'Puritanism run mad' (Ibid, 172), while Winston Churchill would call it 'an affront to the whole history of mankind' (Ibid, 172) and 'at once comic and pathetic' (Ibid, 185). Aside from the obvious fact that Trump is a notorious teetotaler, I believe that many structural parallels can be drawn between today's MAGA movement and the crusade of Prohibition. By this I mean that the parallels are not of a substantive kind, for the simple reason that MAGA is not a reaction to any kind of poison or dangerous, intoxicating substance – unless we are willing to concede Elon Musk's outlandish theory of the so-called 'woke mind virus'.

As Tocqueville eloquently observed, democratic centuries sometimes overdo it with their obsession over equality, even to the extent that it can turn into a form of orthodoxy among liberals. But whether metaphorical intoxication or true political commitment to a bona fides principle of the Enlightenment – *égalité* – the reaction to such a political force has come in the form of a violent backlash, just as militant and inflexible as Prohibition once was. Enter MAGA, *'le delirium anti-woke'*. The structural parallels I speak of can be found, first, in MAGA's composition. Just like the Prohibition movement, MAGA in 2025 is a strange collection of political forces, almost the exact same as those who a century ago rallied behind the 'dry' banner. Indeed, MAGA has its own racists, nativists, and populists. If not the female suffragists of old, MAGA at least commands the loyalty of another perceived disenfranchised gendered group of our day – young male voters, or the so-called 'bro-vote'. As for progressives, they are represented by the techno-futurist elements of the MAGA movement, led by Elon Musk (not unlike another antisemitic automobile magnate who supported the drys, Henry Ford).

On the opposite side of the aisle, the Democrats of today find themselves in a similar situation to that of the 'wets' of the last century: 'Disorganized, dysfunctional, and disbelieving, the wets had watched the approach of Prohibition (…) "in a dumb stupor"' (Ibid, 113).

Second, in terms of its lifespan, the MAGA movement can be said to have been five decades in the making before it got into the halls of federal power in Washington D.C., just like Prohibition found its way into the most sacred document of the land, the US Constitution, since its humble origins in the 1870s when the first bills were proposed and rejected (Ibid, 62). Similarly, the intellectual origins of the MAGA movement have been traced back to an obscure, yet momentous, memorandum published in 1971 by a conservative lawyer, Lewis F. Powell (Powell 1971). This manifesto, which ends with an ominous closing ('the hour is late'), decries an open assault on the American economic system by socialism, communism and fascism. It further highlights the importance of reconquering universities and the media as neglected spaces by conservatives. The Powell Memo is said to have inspired the infamous 'Project 2025' document that the Trump administration is striving to implement (Heer 2024). A seed planted in 1971 and bearing fruit in 2025. A long fever dream indeed.

Will the MAGA lifespan equal that of the Prohibition movement, that is, more than half a century from the time the first dry amendments were proposed in the 1870s until the 21st Amendment finally repealed the 18th Amendment in 1933? It is hard to tell. Since MAGA and Trumpism are now a phenomenon that transcends the life of a sole individual, it is safe to assume that after Donald Trump leaves office the movement will stay strong and live on – probably carried forward on the shoulders of J.D. Vance. And MAGA has not even attempted to enact a constitutional amendment at the time of writing, an accomplishment that, if successful, would equal the Prohibition feat of inserting an illiberal pathogen into an otherwise liberal host.

What happens after that, and how MAGA ends, is also something difficult to predict, not least because predictions can be wrong, almost comically so as Okrent also reminds us:

> In September 1930 Morris Sheppard, author of the Eighteenth Amendment, said, "There is as much chance of repealing the Eighteenth Amendment as there is for a hummingbird to fly to the planet Mars with the Washington Monument tied to its tail". (...) It was one of those moments when all the experts are wrong and wisdom arises from unlikely sources (Ibid, 330).

Whether we draw our lessons from any of these un-American experiments (Prohibition, Fascism, or the Red Scare), or from all of them, and whatever 'un-American' means in substantive terms, methodologically there is one thing that cannot be up for debate: no *one* person in the US has or should have the power to designate another person as un-American in keeping with that country's own democratic tradition. It is, ultimately, a collective decision made over generations. As the Supreme Court decided decades ago: 'The very nature of our free government makes it completely incongruous to have a rule of law under which a group of citizens temporarily in office can deprive another group of citizens of their citizenship' (US Supreme Court 1967).

The Anti-Antonines: 'Malice Toward All'

Perhaps it is inaccurate and misleading to call these experiments 'un-American'. After all, they have all been homebrewed. No alien or external force possessed Americans to ban alcohol, flirt with fascism, or hunt down suspected communists. Could it be that there is something underneath the marbled halls of neo-classic Washington DC, something lurking in the shadows behind the scenes of the great constitutional drama that has been put on display for the past 250 years?

When trying to make sense of similarly dark days in a supposedly highly civilized place, a refugee from Nazi Germany came up with an explanation as to how an otherwise sophisticated society, where there is rule of law and science and art thrive, can at the same time produce some of the most monstrous manifestations of our human nature, turbocharged by the totalitarian state. Our refugee, Hannah Arendt, postulated that after World War II: 'The subterranean stream of Western history has finally come to the surface and usurped the dignity of our tradition' (Arendt 1962, ix). She was specifically referring to the unholy alliance between antisemitism, imperialism, and totalitarianism (Ibid), all of which converged to maximum catastrophic effect in the 1930s and 1940s.

Is there an equivalent 'subterranean stream' in US history? Antisemitism has its own record in the US, and its instrumentalization for political gain (for instance, by the Trump administration in its feud against Harvard University) does not belie the fact of its existence in the country. And totalitarianism, arguably the most sophisticated form of illiberalism harnessing all the tools at the disposal of the modern state, is something the US has flirted with in the past (for example, with the concentration camps where thousands of citizens of Japanese descent were forcibly interned during World War II).

However, there is another subterranean stream that runs deep beneath the tides of American history. Its roots are medieval, yet its manifestations are modern. It combines the worst of all traditions. It refers to the way politics are conducted in that country, a tradition that does not begin with Trump but arguably culminates in his rise to power. It can be characterized as the opposite of the spirit of reconciliation and magnanimity towards defeated enemies, the 'malice toward none' creed of President Abraham Lincoln (Maddow 2025, 297). With Trump, it becomes the exact opposite: 'malice toward all'.

A scholar of the Middle Ages once described the spirit of medieval times as one of 'passionate intensity of life' (Huizinga 1996, 1), a time when a 'fervent pathos' (Ibid, 9) animated people in everything they did, including politics: 'The blind passion with which a man supported his party and his lord and, at the same time, pursued his own interests was, in part, an expression of an unmistakable, stone-hard sense of right that medieval man thought proper' (Ibid, 20).

I believe that, in some ways, perhaps due to the lack of a war of religion like those Europe once had (the Civil War of 1861–65 in reality an example of modern warfare) the US has still not come out of this medieval frame of mind carried across the Atlantic by the pilgrims and settlers, with its distinctive blind passion and intensity – not least when it comes to the fraught politics of the culture wars (on which I said more in Chapter Six). It is a stylistic medievalism, a 'folk-feudalism' of sorts to go with what has been called 'techno-feudalism' as a system of post-capitalist exploitation (Varoufakis 2024).

Donald Trump epitomizes this folk-feudalistic blind passion. He learned from the very best. Indeed, he was mentored in the dark arts of dirty politics by that

Mephistophelian figure called Roy Cohn, an extremely well-connected and corrupt New York attorney who 'galloped through the second half of the twentieth century like a malevolent Forrest Gump' (Bruney 2020, para. 2). Cohn, in turn, assisted Senator McCarthy in his infamous witch-hunt against alleged communists, known as the Red Scare.

Like his heirs, Cohn and Trump, McCarthy was a controversial character. Risen describes him in a way that would be completely suited for the 47th President of the United States today:

> McCarthy attacked with abandon. He became part of the political landscape, a reliable source for outrageous quotes and a bellwether for the insanity of the moment. Facts, accuracy, and consistency did not matter (Risen 2025, 266).

Concerning Cohn, Risen remarks that he was a distillation of everything people loved about McCarthy: 'his viciousness, his vindictiveness, his willingness to lie' (Ibid, 279). Next in line in this hapless dynasty is Donald Trump, an adoptive son to a vicious political father (Cohn) and adoptive grandson to an equally venomous grandfather (McCarthy). Only time will tell whether the 'talented Mr. Vance' (Packer 2025) will enroll his chameleonic political persona to become next in line after he is done fulfilling his constitutional duties as Vice-President.

Thus, just as Rome had its good Antonine emperors, America got its 'anti-Antonines' spanning a century of national history carried by the subterranean stream of folk-feudalism and periodically emerging on the surface, 'flooding the zone' and mudding the waters as they pervaded everything. It was only a matter of time before these uncontainable hydrodynamic forces started overflowing into the rest of the world.

Trump's Codicil to the Monroe Doctrine: The Reluctant Empire Revisited

Donald Trump is not a learned man. He might be clever – enough to get himself elected President of the United States twice – but he is most certainly not a knowledgeable person. He has been called 'uneducable' by the media, his mind described as 'full of mush' by a former advisor (Irwin 2025). He is an ignorant man, and proudly so. That is why he has no problem picking a fight with one of the oldest, most revered academic institutions of his country, Harvard University, as he has no respect, or need, for knowledge. Further, it is also baffling that his ignorance includes one of the areas where he is supposed to be savvier – business – as he is apparently convinced that tariffs are an entry fee that countries magically send his way for the privilege of doing business with the US instead of the sales tax on the American consumer that they actually are.

Trump's self-assured ignorance extends, of course, to history as well. He does not understand history, and therefore he does not understand how the world works. 'He lives from day to day', in Goethe's words, blithefully unaware of all the many paths the present has taken to come to be. His is not a praeter-colonial mind, not even a colonial one; his is an 'ahistorical mind'. But what does it matter what goes on in the mind of Trump? Reflecting on his first months in office, Zoe Williams has written that: 'One of the many indignities of the US spectacle is having to lose hours analyzing the hidden meaning and augurs of the acts of men who don't, themselves, give one second's thought to anything' (Williams 2025).

Commentators advise to take Donald Trump *seriously*, but *not literally* – a phrase that has become a mantra of our hapless times. I believe, however, that although Trump*ism* must be taken seriously for all of the above-mentioned considerations, a mind as ignorant and impressionable as Trump's must always be taken literally, just like the words of a child, if it is intent what we are inquiring about. *Take Trump literally, and Trumpism seriously.*

It is only when the world offers resistance – with all its annoying facts and laws of physics and economics and politics – that the designs of a childish mind like Trump's are thwarted and he, expectedly, gives up or moves on to the next shiny object in sight. A mind that does not care or think about history – a mind that has no grasp of the workings of the world around it – is a mind that truly believes that the world can be carved out and remade like a lab experiment or a tragicomic pantomime of the imperial divisions of old. It is a mind that truly believes disputed biblical lands can be turned into a 'riviera of the Middle East'; that historic bodies of water shared with other nations can be renamed at a whim; that he can snatch an entire country from the Commonwealth of Nations and turn it into his 51st state; or seize a chunk of an old northern kingdom all in the name of securing his own hemisphere – that is, his own side of the gameboard.

It is indeed an actively imaginative mind the way only children playing a game of Risk can be. Enter Trump's Codicil to the Monroe Doctrine. President James Monroe declared in 1823 that America would be henceforth for 'Americans' – whether North our South, arguably, and certainly to the exclusion of European imperialism. Subsequently, at the turn of the twentieth century President Teddy Roosevelt added his famous 'Corollary' to the Monroe Doctrine, namely, his willingness to enforce such a doctrine in the hemisphere up to and including the use of force (Allison 2017, 208–209).

Today, Trump keeps a portrait of President James Monroe in the Oval Office, and although he does not truly understand why or what the Monroe Doctrine really is – he has referred to the portrait as *'Monroe from the Monroe document'* – he has accidentally walked down the path of Monroe and Roosevelt before him by following, if not proper foreign policy principles, at least his blind, predatory impulses telling him to grab as much as he can of everything in his immediate vicinity.

This is Trump's, and MAGA's, own version of imperialism (Collinson 2025), admittedly a continuation of an expansionist tradition dating back to the days of 'Manifest Destiny' (the doctrine underpinning US expansion westward) and even Oliver Cromwell's 'Irish Tactics' to subdue neighboring Ireland and 'Western Design' to take the Americas from Spain in the seventeenth century (Grandin 2025, 85; 106).

Thus, Trump's neo-imperialist inclinations towards everything located in his immediate sphere of influence, the Western Hemisphere, has so far spared no one – not Panama, not Mexico, not Colombia, not Greenland, not even as close an economic and political ally as Canada. Since his ahistorical mind believes these are not real countries with real borders, and that the world around him can be redrawn at a whim, there is no need to acknowledge the basic fact of the sovereignty or territorial integrity of any of them. The same applies for other (real or perceived) powerful countries in their own 'spheres of influence' – a doctrinal concept that is making a comeback in international relations (Foreign Policy 2025) – namely China and Russia. That is why Trump does not really care about Ukraine, or about Taiwan for that matter.

To reiterate: Trump and his followers do not care about history or facts. That is also why he will likely continue to throw ridiculous distractions at the American public exploiting longstanding pop culture obsessions, like the Kennedy assassination or the Fort Knox gold. Conceivably, before his term is up, he will dangle more such stories at the public, for example UFOs in Roswell, New Mexico; or treating Cuba, which is dangerously close to his beloved Mar-a-Lago residence, as a place that needs to be 'liberated' from its own history. These things may never come to pass; but if they do, none of us will be surprised. Anything is possible.

In a way, the ahistorical mind is the opposite of the praeter-colonial mind. The former is tragically unaware of colonialism and its impact on the present, whereas the latter tries to make sense of all of colonialism's many legacies and checkered past. Yet, that does not mean that the ahistorical mind cannot accommodate paradoxes. In fact, it is a place where contradiction thrives, where a bi-polar empire fits perfectly well within a multi-polar world.

Otherwise, how could it be explained that America must be made great *again* (the implication being: that America was once great, and that this is no longer the case), and at the same time that it already is the greatest country? How to make sense of demands for equal treatment after decades of the world 'ripping America off' while at the same time believing it is indeed a country that deserves special treatment, special respect? Only in a paradoxical mind can greatness and equality be both true at the same time. As Zakaria notes:

> The United States has always had two fundamental attitudes. One, we are too good to participate in the world. Or we are so good that we should completely transform the world. But to actually engage in the world as it exists has always been difficult for the United States because it's an ideological nation. It believes it is exceptional and all that. And I think you see some of that in the Trump attitude (Klein and Zakaria 2025, para. 192).

Further, the ahistorical mind truly believes that America can thrive in splendid isolation and at the same time dictate what others can or cannot do, at least when it comes to its own sphere of influence, but certainly also beyond that space. However, by definition, an empire cannot remain in isolation.

Isolation is further negative for the world the US helped to build for the past eight decades, as pointed out by a Republican hawk like Condoleezza Rice during the last presidential race (Rice 2024). Such an order has, others believe, greatly benefited the country that exists at its very center, the US (Klein and Zakaria 2025). It is not that the US was not imperialistic while building and enforcing such a world order; but, as Grandin points out, it managed to navigate this contradiction without hypocrisy by way of 'figuring the most efficient mix ... of empire and law, domination and arbitration – of going alone and working together' (Grandin 2025, 330). Trump's bulldozer-like approach to the international negates this very legacy.

One of the main architects of the post-war order, Truman's Secretary of State, Dean Acheson, titled his memoirs *Present at the Creation,* complete with an epigraph by Alphonso X, the Learned of Spain: 'Had I been present at the creation I would have given some useful hints for the better ordering of the universe' (Acheson 1987). Present at the dismantling of the same order, it seems Donald the Builder can't be bothered with any hints or advice to aid him in the cavalier destruction he is presiding over.

The New Athenians

At the Shangri-La Dialogue event held in Singapore between May and June of 2025, the host Defense Minister addressed the following message to his American counterpart, Pete Hegseth, playing the Melian islander to his Athenian ambassador:

> If we have to choose sides, may we choose the side of principles — principles that uphold a global order where we do not descend into the law of the jungle, where the mighty do what they wish and the weak suffer what they must (Tharoor 2025, para. 15).

In the age of Trump, however, such lofty language is probably completely lost on the likes of Hegseth, Rubio, Vance, or Trump himself. What these new Athenians have in common is not only that they are all men; it is the new brand of masculinity that they celebrate, promote and bring to the table of diplomatic affairs that is interesting, if not for its originality, at least for the perils it entails.

Indeed, we have seen this style of what Zakaria calls 'macho realism' (Klein and Zakaria 2025, para. 250) before in the US, in an iteration brought to us by another one of those spawns of McCarthyism, Richard Nixon. In his 1975 book *The Male Machine* (complete with an Introduction by the iconic feminist thinker Gloria Steinem), Marc Feigen Fasteau included a chapter titled 'Vietnam and the Cult of Toughness in Foreign Policy' where he summarizes this style of macho diplomacy as follows:

> In short, the search for "peace with honor" in Vietnam, after Kissinger's sophisticated intellectual gloss and skilled diplomatic tactics are stripped away, was shaped and governed by the same tired, dangerous, arbitrary, and "masculine" first principles: one must never back away once a line is drawn in the dust; every battle must be won; and, if one fails to observe the first two injunctions and by some fluke the rest of the world doesn't care, the domestic right – the "real men" – will get you for being too soft (Fargen Fasteau 1975, 180).

This is very similar to what Acheson reports is the Soviet style of diplomacy, the same style today's Russia seems to follow in its negotiations on the war against Ukraine. According to Acheson, the Soviets were not compelled by eloquence or reasoned arguments, but only by the 'calculation of forces':

> Theirs is a more primitive form of political method. They cling stubbornly to a position, hoping to force an opponent to accept it. When and if action by the opponent demonstrates the Soviet position to be untenable, they hastily abandon it – after asking and having been refused an unwarranted price – and hastily take up a new position, which may or may not represent a move toward greater mutual stability (Acheson 1987, 274).

The resemblance between the Soviet (and Russian) way of negotiating and Trump's absurd tariff wars of the present is simply uncanny. The echoes of the Nixonian 'mad man theory' (i.e. calculated unpredictability) in conducting international affairs can also be seen in Trump's approach.

Further, there is more to MAGA diplomacy than just residual Cold War macho energy. There is also a critical entertainment value to it. Historian Niall Ferguson calls it 'Reality TV Politik' (Ferguson 2025). Trump's background as a TV star before politics is, of course, sufficiently known, including his active involvement in the worlds of professional wrestling and mixed martial arts. Testosterone infused and male dominated, there is something of the theatrical in both. Particularly in wrestling, the concept of 'kayfabe' becomes crucial, that is the understanding that everything that goes on between the different 'characters' is taken as genuine – no matter how little or no clothes the emperor dons on the ring.

This performativity in Trump's and MAGA political style was vociferously decried during the 2024 presidential race by journalist Craig Copetas, who even called for the serious media to stop covering then candidate Trump altogether given the artificiality of his entire campaign. Like Tom Crooks, however, Copetas was vastly ignored and his message forgotten.

Stop the Planet – We Want Off!

In 1958, a decade before the first human being set foot on the Moon, Hannah Arendt manifested her perplexity at the eagerness her fellow Earthlings displayed to leave the planet. She commented on the excitement around a human-made satellite orbiting the planet, reportedly a 'first step toward escape from men's imprisonment to the earth' (Arendt 1998, 1). She did not understand why people where so eager to leave a place so essential to our human condition:

> Although Christians have spoken of the earth as a vale of tears and philosophers have looked upon their body as a

prison of mind or soul, nobody in the history of mankind has
ever conceived of the earth as a prison for men's bodies or
shown such eagerness to go literally from here to the moon.
Should the emancipation and secularization of the modern
age, which began with a turning-away, not necessarily from
God, but from a god who was the Father of men in heaven,
end with an even more fateful repudiation of an Earth who was
the Mother of all living creatures under the sky? (Ibid, 2).

Fast forward to our present, what can the praeter-colonial mind do in light of
all of these ominous developments, whereby the most powerful country in the
world is dismantling the world order it helped create and ostensibly retreating
to its inner citadel – not without rekindling old ideas about spheres of
influence and regional imperialism?

The rest of us, that is humanity, all those who have been axiomatically made
a second priority by way of 'America First', will just have to wait and see what
happens after Trump, and Trumpism, spend out their Prohibition-like
momentum. We may have to host some political and intellectual refugees as
well, like the Yale professors fleeing fascism, although it is more likely that
most Americans will stay put hoping they still get to, to quote comedian Dave
Chappelle, 'wear the Nikes and not make them'. Some are optimistic that,
after the trade wars, more sound economic policies will return (Galloway
2025). Others are more pessimistic in light of the political polarization in the
US, even referring to the different social worlds where people inhabit as
'Earth One' and 'Earth Two' (MSNBC 2023). But there is really one planet
Earth, and we are stuck in it for the time being. Or are we?

There is one person who is actively working on trying to get us off this planet
before we ruin it completely: Elon Musk. Just like the Prohibitionist Henry
Ford started his own political experiment in the Amazon in the late 1920s, an
industrial citadel called 'Fordlandia' (Lost in Context 2025), Musk has created
a new administrative unit in the south of Texas to build his own gateway into
Mars. This new 'Cádiz' (the main port from where hundreds of Spanish
vessels departed to the Americas to build an empire) is called 'Starbase'
(Laughland 2025). Perhaps before rushing towards a new planet that we will
surely also ruin (considering human nature is a 'firmware' problem that we
carry within us wherever we go), it might be better to reflect on how we got to
this particular point in time and what it means for us by exercising the
faculties of the praeter-colonial mind. As Arendt prompted us all those
decades ago: 'What I propose, therefore, is very simple: it is nothing more
than to think what we are doing' (Arendt 1998, 5).

Epilogue: The House of the Post-Colonial Spirits

This intellectual journey across the back alleys of empire has been kept deliberately short, as it is the 'simple, practical, and catchy' philosophy that lasts (McDarrah 2024). In such a short space no definitive conclusive argument has been attempted of the kind that puts an end to all dialogue and reflection because it is so compelling. Rather, the aim of this study has been to function as a prompt to get a conversation started, not only with our friends, family, colleagues or even strangers, but just as important, to begin a conversation with ourselves (Arendt 1976, 476), to help our minds better navigate those backstreets we know lie behind the clear-cut constructs inviting us in.

In this sense, this is also not an apology or justification of all the evils of colonialism, as it would be very easy to simply declare with a shrug that 'everything is praeter-colonial and there's nothing we can do'. Rather, the praeter-colonial mind inquires 'if everything is pre-colonial, colonial, and post-colonial all at once, how can I make sense of it all?' It is further not an attempt at 'weaponizing the intellect' (Galeotti 2023, 11) to set a political agenda or an ideological manifesto calling people to action. On the contrary, this is a call to reflect and to live an examined life, to probe our prejudices and assumptions and take with us only what rings true, much as the prudent traveler who strictly packs only what they cannot part with. The rest of our luggage we should leave behind, or pray someone loses it for us.

One of the champions of 'decolonizing the mind' whose work I have used in this study, Kenyan novelist Ngũgĩ wa Thiong'o, believes that language has a dual character, as 'it is both a means of communication and a carrier of culture' (Thiong'o 2005, 12). For example, English is spoken the world over, but when it is used by non-native English speakers like Swedish and Danish (or Chilean) people, it can only serve the first function, namely it can only work as a means of communication when said peoples engage with others who do not speak their native tongue. For English speakers, conversely, this language serves a dual function, both as a means for communicating with non-native English speakers, while at the same time carrying the particular culture of the native speakers, most distinctively the British (Ibid, 13).

Thiong'o further contends that language as culture has three important aspects. First, culture (and its articulation, language) is a product of history. Second, language as culture is an 'image-forming' agent in the mind of a child – a device for identity-building. Third, although speech is a universal human ability, 'a specific culture is not transmitted through language in its universality but in its particularity as the language of a specific community with a specific history' (Ibid, 15).

In other words, all humans are endowed with the ability to speak, but once destiny assigns them their first language, they are forever stuck in this accidental pigeonhole in which alone they can truly experience their culture, and as result, their own identity. Thus, the argument goes that only native speakers can carry their own culture and history in that first language – assuming that there are no bilingual or multilingual cultures, which is of course counter-factual as we know of many such cultures. Consequently, anyone attempting to express culture in a language other than those assigned to them as a child must be confused, alienated, pretending, or flat out lying. I beg to differ. Many phenomena in today's world are being experienced, designated and rationalized by people in English even if this is not their native tongue.

For example, there is not one specific word in Spanish for 'accountability' (the closest would be '*rendición de cuentas*') but the English word has nonetheless entered the vernacular of Spanish speakers around the world, not only as a phoneme but also as a way of life in the fight against corruption. Another example is *Gairaigo*, or the set of Japanese words borrowed from foreign languages, especially from English, that have become part of that nation's identity, such as '*anime*' (from 'animation') and '*tekunorojī*' (from 'technology'). And it would be nothing short of insulting to tell a Ukrainian 'drone operator' ('оператор дрона') that he or she is culturally confused or is faking an Anglo-Saxon identity by identifying themselves as a user of an Anglo-Saxon concept ('drone') as they shoulder the burden of defending an entire nation.

Language is, therefore, much richer as a vehicle for culture(s) than Thiong'o would give it credit for. The triumph of one language, English, that originally belonged to one culture, the Anglo-Saxons, as a carrier of thoughts and experiences accessible today to every person on Earth is proof that language needs not be this rigid, or culture that parochial. After all, if Thiong'o was right and there would be no way of experiencing culture outside of our own native language, then humanity would have, out of necessity, found a way to make work those scientific languages that do not belong to one single culture or civilization but that are devised as a summary of them all, such as Esperanto. But you are not reading this in Esperanto now, are you?

More personally, I have experienced first-hand what it feels like to carry and express culture in a language other than my native tongue. Indeed, although not rightfully mine by birth, English has come to be the vehicle through which I have been afforded the privilege of becoming a family man, as it is the language of my wife and of our son. The praeter-colonial mind cannot but rejoice in the fact that the condition of possibility for love and family for us children of post-colonial spaces from North and South America is the legacy of an empire that never reached the shores where I was born. My wife and my son are now my kin, blood of my blood, and I cannot fake our bond any more than I can pretend a feeling is truly real if I only use the words spoken by my forebearers to express it. However, I had to express this exclusively in Spanish, I would borrow a line from a Spaniard traveling across modern Ukraine whose people forever stole his heart, and declare that, in all truthfulness, '*ellos se convirtieron en mi gente*' (Lasheras 2022, 337) ('they became my people').

The power of these cultural spirits can further be felt beyond the confines of our home; they have also allowed our praeter-colonial minds to get a glimpse of entire new-old worlds, not least in all those post-Soviet/post-colonial spaces, like Ukraine, where Russian is not always spoken or even welcome anymore. In such places, English serves not only as means of communication, but also as a way to keep alive an old cultural legacy that began precisely in the pastoral life of ancient Ukraine, as Timothy Snyder reminds us, since it was there that all Indo-European languages, including English and Spanish, were born (Snyder 2024).

We began this journey by talking about Ukraine's war of national liberation against the yoke of Russian imperialism. Indeed, Russia today has been characterized as something the praeter-colonial mind may find not too difficult to understand, namely 'a postmodern empire, in which many of the physical features of empire have disappeared, but where the imperial spirit is still present and even resurgent' (Stent 2023, 180). The problem is, this spirit has actually materialized in a most violent way with Russia's war of aggression against Ukraine. For Ukrainians, this is a fight for their own existence as a nation and will continue to be so for generations to come, until they reach the blessed state of affairs where they can again break bread with their former colonizers in peace, just as our Pan-American family can today with the sons and daughters of our former European masters. Woefully, it might just take a while for them to get there.

We also began this journey by looking at some of the meanings of the word 'praeter', including the 'past' and at the same time what lies 'beyond'. In that sense, Ukraine's transcendent clamor for freedom today is an echo from the past of any independent nation that once fought and bled for its own existence, a reminder of what we all once were and how far we have come since. And so, as we find ourselves back home again, while my wife takes a call from Kyiv, our son hums *Carol of the Bells* (A Ukrainian Christmas carol), and I read a book on Ukraine's history, I treasure our little Ukrainian moment as these post-colonial echoes perfectly encapsulate all the wondrous things history has to offer to those whose minds are wise enough not to lose sight of the past and whose hearts remain open to all the many possibilities of the future.

References

Acemoglu, D. and Robinson, J. 2012. *Why Nations Fail. The Origins of Power, Prosperity, and Poverty.* Penguin Random House.

Acheson, Dean. 1987. *Present at the Creation.* W.W. Norton & Company.

Ackerman, E. and Stavridis, J. 2021. *2034: A Novel of the Next World War.* Penguin.

Adams, John. 1789. "John Adams to Thomas Boylston Adams." *Founders Archives*, September 2. https://founders.archives.gov/documents/Adams/04-08-02-0218

Alice Lan, Alice. 2023. "TikTok has its problems, but Sinophobia doesn't answer them." *Scot Scoop,* April 7. https://scotscoop.com/column-tiktok-has-its-problems-but-sinophobia-is-not-the-answer/

Allison, Graham. 2017. *Destined for War. Can America and China Escape Thucydides' Trap?* Houghton Mifflin Harcourt.

Allison, Graham. 2018. "The Myth of the Liberal Order: From Historical Accident to Conventional Wisdom." *Foreign Affairs* 97 (4): 124–133.

Álvarez, Alejandro. 1922. *International Law and Related Subjects From the Point of View of the American Continent.* Carnegie Endowment for International Peace.

Amnesty International. 2021. "China's Mass Internment, Torture and Persecution of Muslims in Xinjiang." *Amnesty International*, June 10. https://xinjiang.amnesty.org/

Anderson, Mark. 2013. "Hanged on a comma: drafting can be a matter of life and death." *IP Draughts*, October 14. https://ipdraughts.wordpress.com/2013/10/14/hanged-on-a-comma-drafting-can-be-a-matter-of-life-and-death/

Andrew, N., Cleven, N. and Thornton, William. 1932. "Thornton's Outlines of a Constitution for United North and South Columbia." *The Hispanic American Historical Review* 12 (2): 198–215.

Arendt, Hannah. 1961. *Between Past and Future*. Viking Press.

Arendt, Hannah. 1962. *The Origins of Totalitarianism.* Meridian.

Arendt, Hannah. 1998. *The Human Condition.* Chicago University Press.

Arendt, Hannah. 2006. *Eichmann in Jerusalem. A Report on the Banality of Evil.* Penguin.

Armstrong, Stephen. 2006. "Mohamed Al Fayed Interview: Pharaos Revenge." *The Guardian*, April 15. https://www.theguardian.com/commentisfree/2006/apr/15/comment.mainsection3

Arshad, Rowena. 2021. "Decolonising the curriculum – how do I get started?" *THE*, September 14. https://www.timeshighereducation.com/campus/decolonising-curriculum-how-do-i-get-started

Asimov, Isaac. 2004. *I, Robot*. Bantam Dell.

Australian Defence Forces. 2021. "Afghanistan Inquiry Report." *ADF,* n/d. https://www.defence.gov.au/sites/default/files/2021-10/IGADF-Afghanistan-Inquiry-Public-Release-Version.pdf

Becker Lorca, Arnulf. 2015. *Mestizo International Law.* Cambridge University Press.

Beinart, Peter. 2021. "The Vacuous Phrase at the Core of Biden's Foreign Policy." The New York Times, June 22. https://www.nytimes.com/2021/06/22/opinion/biden-foreign-policy.html

Benton, Lauren. 2024. *They Called It Peace. Worlds of Imperial Violence.* Princeton University Press.

Bildt, Carl. 2024. "A Hillbilly Elegy for Ukraine and the West." *Project Syndicate,* July 23. https://www.project-syndicate.org/commentary/vance-trump-abandon-ukraine-cede-power-to-russia-china-elsewhere-by-carl-bildt-2024-07

Binet, Laurent. 2021. *Civilizations.* Picador.

Black Rebellion. 2025. "Africa Will Not Kneel." *Black Rebellion,* May 17. https://www.youtube.com/watch?v=0tJNwtEp0dU

Bolaño, Roberto. 2016. *La literatura nazi en América*. Penguin.

Borges, J.L. 1943. "Poema Conjetural." *Revista Altazor*, n/d. https://www.revistaaltazor.cl/jorge-luis-borges-poema-conjetural/

Bregman, Rutger. 2021. *Humankind. A Hopeful History*. Bloomsbury Publishing.

Brook, Timothy. 2009. *Vermeer's Hat.* Profile Books.

Bruney, Gabrielle. 2020. "Roy Cohn Was an Infamous Political Fixer Who Made President Trump "From Beyond the Grave." *Esquire,* June 18. https://www.esquire.com/entertainment/a29177110/wheres-my-roy-cohn-matt-tyrnauer-donald-trump-interview/

Brunstetter, D. and Lobo, F. 2024. "R2P, the Imperial Critique, and Self-Determination: Recovering the Narrative of the Tlaxcaltecas." *Global Responsibility to Protect*: 1–26.

Brunstetter, Daniel and Zartner, Dana. 2011. "Just War against Barbarians: Revisiting the Valladolid Debates between Sepúlveda and Las Casas." *Political Studies* 59(3): 733–752.

Buttigieg, Pete. 2025. "We Are Still Underreacting on AI." *Pete Buttigieg's Substack*, June 24. https://petebuttigieg.substack.com/p/we-are-still-underreacting-on-ai

Carmagnani, Marcello. 2011. *The Other West: Latin America from Invasion to Globalization* University of California Press.

Carroll, James. 2002. *Constantine's Sword. The Church and the Jews*. Mariner Books.

Center for AI Safety. 2023. "Statement on AI risk." *Center for AI Safety*, May 30. https://www.safe.ai/statement-on-ai-risk

Chaudhuri, Amit. 2016. "The Real Meaning of Rhodes must Fall." *The Guardian*, March 16. https://www.theguardian.com/uk-news/2016/mar/16/the-real-meaning-of-rhodes-must-fall

Chesterman, Simon. 2025. "Silicon Sovereigns: Artificial Intelligence, International Law, and the Tech-Industrial Complex." *NUS Law Working Paper* No 2025/008.

Chimni, B.S. 2006. "Third World Approaches to International Law: A Manifesto." *International Community Law Review* 8 (3): 3–27.

China Military Online. 2022. "China's increasing contributions to UN peacekeeping operations". *China Military Online,* August 29. http://eng. chinamil.com.cn/CHINA_209163/TopStories_209189/10181314.html

Choudhury, A., and Heiduk, F. 2019. "Aung San Suu Kyi at the International Court of Justice." *SWP-Berlin,* December 18. https://www.swp-berlin. org/10.18449/2019C51/

Clausewitz, Carl von. 2007. *On War.* Oxford University Press.

CNN. 2017. "Donald Trump's Puerto Rico Visit." *CNN,* October 3. https:// edition.cnn.com/2017/10/03/politics/donald-trump-puerto-rico-visit/index.html

CNN. 2025a. "AI CEO explains the terrifying new behavior AIs are showing." *CNN,* June 4. https://www.youtube.com/watch?v=GJeFoEw9x0M

CNN. 2025b. "AI expert: 'We'll be toast' without changes in AI technology." *CNN,* August 14. https://www.youtube.com/ watch?v=IidpM2DsrBE&list=WL&index=35

Collinson, Stephen. 2025. "Trump's threats to Greenland, Canada and Panama explain everything about America First." CNN, January 8. https:// edition.cnn.com/2025/01/08/politics/trump-greenland-canada-panama-analysis/index.html

Conrad, Joseph. 2002a. "An Outpost of Progress." In *Heart of Darkness and Other Tales* by Joseph Conrad. Oxford University Press.

Conrad, Joseph. 2002b. "Heart of Darkness." In *Heart of Darkness and Other Tales* by Joseph Conrad. Oxford University Press.

Cordall, Simon. 2025. "Is Trump the end of the international rules-based order?" *Al Jazeera*, March 16. https://www.aljazeera.com/news/2025/3/16/ is-trump-the-end-of-the-international-rules-based-order

Crichton, Michael. 1976. *Eaters of the Dead*. Knopf.

Darwall, Stephen. 1977. "Two Kinds of Respect." *Ethics* 88:1: 36–49.

De Grazia, Victoria. 2006. *Irresistible Empire. America's Advance through Twentieth-Century Europe.* Harvard University Press.

De Tocqueville, Alexis. 2009. *Democracy in America. Vol II.* Floating Press.

De Vries, Erik. 2001. "Alexandre Kojève-Carl Schmitt Correspondence and Alexandre Kojève, 'Colonialism from a European Perspective'." *Interpretation* 29 (1): 115–130.

Dikeç, Mustafa. 2010. "Colonial Minds, Postcolonial Places." *Antipode* 42 (4): 801–805.

DSEI Japan. 2025. "DSEI Japan 2025: "Today's Ukraine could be East Asia tomorrow", Japan's PM says." *DSEI Japan*, May 22. https://www.dsei-japan. com/news/dsei-japan-2025-todays-ukraine-east-asia-tomorrow-japans-pm

Duffy, B. and Hewlett, K. 2021. "How culture wars start." *King's College London*, May 24. https://www.kcl.ac.uk/news/how-culture-wars-start

Dunlap, Charles J. 2008. "Lawfare Today: A Perspective." *Yale Journal of International Affairs*: 146–154.

DW. 2024. "Exploited for AI." *DW*, November 12. https://www.dw.com/en/ the-human-cost-of-ai-data-workers-in-the-global-south/video-71025482

Emtseva, Julia. 2022. "Practicing Reflexivity in International Law: Running a Never-Ending Race to Catch Up with the Western International Lawyers." *German Law Journal* 23: 756–768.

Ero, Comfort. 2024. "The Trouble With 'the Global South.' What the West Gets Wrong About the Rest." *Foreign Affairs*, April 1. https://www. foreignaffairs.com/world/trouble-global-south

Eslava, Luis and Pahuja, Sundhya. 2012. "Beyond the (Post)Colonial: TWAIL and the Everyday Life of International Law." *Verfassung und Recht in Übersee VRÜ* 45: 195–221.

Espinosa, Aurelio. 1918. "The Term Latin America." *Hispania* 1 (3): 35–143.

European Commission. 2023. "G7 Leader's Statement on the Hiroshima AI Process." *European Commission*, October 30. https://digital-strategy.ec.europa.eu/en/library/g7-leaders-statement-hiroshima-ai-process

European Commission. 2024. "AI Act." *European Commission*, n/d. https://digital-strategy.ec.europa.eu/en/policies/regulatory-framework-ai

Faisal. 1919. "Arabs Demand Independence at Paris Peace Conference." *Arab Revolt,* n/d. https://arabrevolt.jo/en/milestones-list/arabs-demand-independence-at-paris-peace-conference/.

Fanon, Frantz. 1963. *The Wretched of the Earth.* Grove Press.

Fargen Fasteau, Marc. 1975. *The Male Machine.* Delta.

Ferguson, Niall. 2004. *Colossus. The Rise and Fall of the American Empire.* Allen Lane.

Ferguson, Niall. 2018. "The Myth of the Liberal International Order." *Indian Strategic Studies*, January 30. https://www.strategicstudyindia.com/2018/01/the-myth-of-liberal-international-order.html?m=1

Ferguson, Niall. 2025. "Reality TV Politik." *The Free Press*, June 3. https://www.thefp.com/p/niall-ferguson-trumps-foreign-policy

Fitzgerald, F. Scott. 2001. *The Great Gatsby.* Wordsworth Classics.

Foreign Policy "A Return to Spheres of Influence?" *Foreign Policy*, June 1. https://foreignpolicy.com/2025/06/01/spheres-influence-great-power-competition-trump-geography/

France 24. 2024. "Trump targeted again: How violent is US politics?" *France 24*, September 16. https://www.france24.com/en/tv-shows/the-debate/20240916-trump-targeted-again-how-violent-are-us-politics

Future of Life. 2023. "Pause Giant AI Experiments: An Open Letter." *Future of Life*, March 22. https://futureoflife.org/open-letter/pause-giant-ai-experiments

Galeotti, Mark. 2023. *The Weaponisation of Everything. A Field Guide to the New Way of War.* Yale University Press.

Gallie, W.B. 1956. "Essentially Contested Concepts."' *Proceedings of the Aristotelian Society* 56: 167–198.

Galloway, Scott. 2022. *Adrift.* Penguin.

Galloway, Scott. 2025. "Scott Galloway Predicts Apple Tariff Exemption." *Pivot*, April 13. https://www.youtube.com/shorts/b-ypJAWW-8I

García Márquez, Gabriel. 2017. *Cien Años de Soledad.* Diana.

García Pino, Gonzalo. 2022. "Decálogo de razones de una gran derrota." *CIPER,* September 9. https://www.ciperchile.cl/2022/09/09/decalogo-de-razones-de-una-gran-derrota/

Golding, William. 2012. *The Inheritors.* Faber and Faber.

Golding, William. 2023. *Lord of the Flies.* Pomodoro Books.

Gow, Andrew. 1998. "Gog and Magog on *Mappaemundi* and Early Printed World Maps: Orientalizing Ethnography in the Apocalyptic Tradition." *JEMH* 2 (1): 61–88.

Grandin, Greg. 2025. *America, América. A New History of the New World.* Penguin Press.

Haan, Katherine. 2024. "What Is the Five Eyes Alliance?" *Forbes*, June 4. https://www.forbes.com/advisor/business/what-is-five-eyes/

Harari, Yuval Noah. 2014. *Sapiens. A Brief History of Humankind.* Signal Books.

Harari, Yuval Noah. 2024. *Nexus.* Random House.

Hardt, Michael and Negri, Antonio. 2000. *Empire* Harvard University Press.

Hart, H.L.A. 2012. *The Concept of Law*, 3rd ed. Oxford University Press.

Hathaway, Oona A. 2024. "For the Rest of the World, the U.S. President Has Always Been Above the Law. Americans Will Now Know What a Lack of Accountability Means." *Foreign Affairs*, July 16. https://www.foreignaffairs.com/united-states/rest-world-us-president-has-always-been-above-law

HBO. 2021. "Exterminate All the Brutes." n/d. https://www.hbo.com/exterminate-all-the-brutes

Heer, Jeet. 2024. "The Powell Memo Helped Create Project 2025." *The Nation*, September 6. https://www.thenation.com/article/society/powell-memo-project-2025-plutocracy/

HM Government. 2021. *Global Britain in a competitive age. The Integrated Review of Security, Defence, Development and Foreign Policy*. HM Government.

HM Government. 2023. "Integrated Review Refresh." *HM Government*, n/d. https://www.gov.uk/government/publications/integrated-review-refresh-2023-responding-to-a-more-contested-and-volatile-world/integrated-review-refresh-2023-responding-to-a-more-contested-and-volatile-world

House of Commons, Public Administration Select Committee. 2005. *Government by Inquiry. First Report of Session 2004-05. Vol. I.* House of Commons.

Hoyle, Fred. 2010. *The Black Cloud.* Penguin.

Huizinga, Johan. 1996. *The Autumn of the Middle Ages.* University of Chicago Press.

Huntington, Samuel. 1993. "The Clash of Civilizations?" *Foreign Affairs* 72 (3): 22–49.

IBM. 2023. "What is AI Alignment?" *IBM*, October 18. https://www.ibm.com/think/topics/ai-alignment#:~:text=Artificial%20intelligence%20(AI)%20alignment%20is,technologies%20to%20help%20make%20decisions

Ignatieff, Michael. 1998. *The Warrior's Honor. Ethnic war and the modern conscience.* Holt Paperbacks.

Ignatieff, Michael. 2003. *Empire Lite. Nation-building in Bosnia, Kosovo and Afghanistan* Vintage.

Irwin, Lauren. 2025. "Bolton: Trump's 'mind is full of mush.'" *The Hill*, February 25. https://thehill.com/policy/international/5162455-john-bolton-donald-trump-russia-ukraine-war/

Japaridze, Tinatin. 2022. *Stalin's Millennials.* Lexington Books.

Johnson, Howard. 1978. "The political uses of commissions of enquiry (1): The imperial – colonial West Indies context. The Forster and Moyne commissions." *Social and Economic Studies* 27 (3): 256–283.

Kastner, Ruth E. 2016. "The Quantum and the 'Preternatural'." *Transactional Interpretation,* February 1. https://transactionalinterpretation.org/2016/02/01/the-quantum-and-the-preternatural/

Kaplan, Robert D. 2023. *The Loom of Time. Between Empire and Anarchy, From the Mediterranean to China*. Random House.

Keohane, Robert and Nye, Joseph. 2025. "The End of the Long American Century." *Foreign Affairs*, June 2. https://www.foreignaffairs.com/united-states/end-long-american-century-trump-keohane-nye

Kinsella, Helen M. 2011. *The Image before the Weapon. A Critical History of the Distinction between Combatant and Civilian*. Cornell University Press.

Kissinger, Henry, Mundie, Craig, and Schmidt, Eric. 2024. *Genesis.* Little, Brown and Company.

Klein, Ezra and Zakaria, Fareed. 2025. "The Dark Heart of Trump's Foreign Policy." *The New York Times,* January 3. https://www.nytimes.com/2025/03/01/opinion/ezra-klein-podcast-fareed-zakaria.html

Koskenniemi, Martti. 2011. "Empire and International Law: The Real Spanish Contribution." *University of Toronto Law Journal* 61: 1–36.

Koskenniemi, Martti. 2021. *To the Uttermost Parts of the Earth. Legal Imagination and International Power, 1300-1870*. Cambridge University Press.

Kotlyarevsky, Ivan. 2004. *Aeneid.* The Basilian Press.

Kremlin. 2022. "Joint Statement of the Russian Federation and the People's Republic of China on the International Relations Entering a New Era and the Global Sustainable Development." *Kremlin*, February 4. http://www.en.kremlin.ru/supplement/5770

Kuleba, Dmytro. 2021. "Ukraine Is Part of the West. NATO and the EU Should Treat It That Way." *Foreign Affairs,* August 2. https://www.foreignaffairs.com/ukraine/ukraine-part-west

Kuleba, Dmytro. 2024. "Preface." In *Війна і нові горизонти,* edited by Dmytro Kuleba. Knygolove.

Kuo, Ming-Sung. 2020. "China's Legal Blitzkrieg in Hong Kong". *The Diplomat*, August 8. https://thediplomat.com/2020/08/chinas-legal-blitzkrieg-in-hong-kong

Labuda, Patryk. 2024. "Countering Imperialism in International Law: Examining the Special Tribunal for Aggression Against Ukraine through a Post-Colonial Eastern European Lens."'*The Yale Journal of International Law* 49: 272–310.

Laidlaw, Zoë. 2012. "Investigating Empire: Humanitarians, Reform and the Commission of Eastern Inquiry." *The Journal of Imperial and Commonwealth History* 40 (5): 749–768.

Laikwan, Pang. 2024. *One and All. The Logic of Chinese Sovereignty.* Stanford University Press.

Lambert, Lt Col Claude A. 2024. "Small Eagle, Big Dragon: China's Expanding Role in UN Peacekeeping." *RUSI*, July 19. https://www.rusi.org/explore-our-research/publications/commentary/small-eagle-big-dragon-chinas-expanding-role-un-peacekeeping

Lasheras, Borja. 2022. *Estación Ucrania. El país que fue*. Libros del K.O.

Laughland, Oliver. 2025. "Fear, hope and loathing in Elon Musk's new city: 'It's the wild, wild west and the future.'" *The Guardian*, May 23. https://www.theguardian.com/technology/2025/may/23/elon-musk-new-city-starbase-texas

Lavrova, Masha. 2024. "Historian Jade McGlynn: Putin 100% believes Russia's distorted history." *Kyiv Independent,* March 8. https://kyivindependent.com/putin-100-believes-russias-distorted-history

Lévy, Bernard-Henri. 2019. *The Empire and the Five Kings. America's Abdication and the Fate of the World*. Holt Paperbacks.

Liang, Qiao and Xiangsui, Wang. 1999. *Unrestricted Warfare.* PLA Literature and Arts Publishing House.

Liddy, Major Lynda. 2005. "The Strategic Corporal. Some requirements in training and education." *Australian Army Journal,* II (2): 139–148.

Lindqvist, Sven. 2018. *Exterminate All the Brutes*. Granta.

Lobo, Francisco. 2015. "Exposing torture – the virtue of American hypocrisy." *Open Democracy*, January 15. https://www.opendemocracy.net/en/openglobalrights-openpage-blog/exposing-torture-virtue-of-american-hypocrisy/

Lobo, Francisco. 2021. "¿Quién es Chile? Colo-Colo, los Redskins, Aunt Jemima y la Negrita." *El Mostrador,* July 27. https://www.elmostrador.cl/noticias/opinion/columnas/2021/07/27/quien-es-chile-colo-colo-los-redskins-aunt-jemima-y-la-negrita/

Lobo, Francisco. 2023. "Defending the Rules-Based Order: The US at a Crossroads." *RUSI*, March 28. https://rusi.org/explore-our-research/publications/commentary/defending-rules-based-order-us-crossroads

Lobo, Francisco. 2024. "The Quest for the Ukrainian '*Araucana*': The Case for the Humanization of the Orc." *Revista Electrónica Iberoamericana* 18 (2).

Lobo, Francisco. 2025. "Alonso de la Vera Cruz (1507-1584)." In *Just War Thinkers Revisited,* edited by Daniel Brunstetter and Cian O'Driscoll. Routledge.

Lost in Context. 2025. "Henry Ford vs. The Amazon." Lost in Context, February 9. https://www.youtube.com/watch?v=yHjqEj9w0UA

Louis, William Roger. 1964. "Roger Casement and the Congo." *The Journal of African History* 5 (1): 99–120.

- Lupher, David. 2009. *Romans in a New World. Classical Models in Sixteenth-Century Spanish America*. The University of Michigan Press.

Maçães, Bruno. 2019. *Belt and Road. A Chinese World Order*. Hurst & Co.

Maddow, Rachel. 2023. *Prequel. An American Fight Against Fascism.* Crown Publishing Group.

Maher, Bill. 2024. *What This Comedian Said Will Shock You.* Simon & Schuster.

Maier-Katkin, B. and Maier-Katkin, D. 2004. "At the Heart of Darkness: Crimes against Humanity and the Banality of Evil." *Human Rights Quarterly* 26 (3): 584–604.

Massad, Joseph. 2015. "Orientalism and Occidentalism." *History of the Present* 5 (1): 83–94.

Mayer, Jane. *The Dark Side*. Doubleday.

McDarrah, Theodore. 2024. "Simple, Practical, And Catchy: The Philosophy That Lasts." *Forbes*, May 31. https://www.forbes.com/sites/teddymcdarrah/2024/05/31/simple-practical-and-catchy-the-philosophy-that-lasts/?sh=127c59ab2341

Menocal, María Rosa. 2003. *The Ornament Of The World: How Muslims, Jews, and Christians Created a Culture of Tolerance in Medieval Spain*. Little, Brown and Company.

Mignolo, Walter D. 2017. "Coloniality Is Far from Over, and So Must Be Decoloniality." *Afterall* 43: 38–45.

Mikhnovsky, Mykola. 1996. "An In dependent Ukraine." In *Towards an Intellectual History of Ukraine* edited by Ralph Lindheim and George S.N. Luckyj. University of Toronto Press.

MMU. 2024. "Decolonising the Curriculum Toolkit." *MMU*, n/d. https://www.mmu.ac.uk/about-us/professional-services/uta/reducing-awarding-gaps/decolonising-the-curriculum-toolkit

Modirzadeh, Naz. 2023. "'Let Us All Agree to Die a Little': TWAIL's Unfulfilled Promise." *Harvard International Law Journal* 65 (1): 79–131.

MSNBC. 2023. "Nicolle: 'Gap between Earth 1 and Earth 2 on full display' as Garland defends DOJ in hearing." *MSNBC*, September 21. https://www. youtube.com/watch?v=hpbZ4ayOe4k

Müller, Martin. 2018. "In Search of the Global East: Thinking between North and South." *Geopolitics* 25 (3): 734–755.

NATO. 2018. "The Atlantic Charter." *NATO,* July 2. https://www.nato.int/cps/ en/natohq/official_texts_16912.htm

NATO. 2024. "Washington Summit Declaration." *NATO*, July 10. https://www. nato.int/cps/en/natohq/official_texts_227678.htm

New Zealand Army. 2020. "The Way of the New Zealand Warrior." *New Zealand Army*, n/d. https://www.nzdf.mil.nz/assets/Uploads/DocumentLibrary/ Way-of-the-New-Zealand-Warrior-2020.pdf

Ng, Andrew. 2017. "Why AI Is the New Electricity." *GSB*, March 11. https:// www.gsb.stanford.edu/insights/Andrew-ng-why-ai-new-electricity

Okrent, Daniel. 2010. *Last Call: The Rise and Fall of Prohibition.* Scribner.

Oxford English Dictionary. 2024. "Praeter." n/d. https://www.oed.com/ dictionary/preter_prefix?tab=etymology#28250378

Packer, George. 2025. 'The Talented Mr. Vance." *The Atlantic,* May 19. https://www.theatlantic.com/magazine/archive/2025/07/jd-vance-reinvention-power/682828/

Pamuk, Ohran. 2011. *The Black Book.* Faber and Faber.

Parker, Philip. 2022. *The Atlas of Atlases.* Ivy Press.

Patrikarakos, David. 2017. *War in 140 Characters. How Social Media Is Reshaping Conflict in the Twenty-First Century.* Basic Books.

Pérez Rosales, Vicente. 1886. *Recuerdos del Pasado. 1814-1860.* Imprenta Gutenberg.

Pesek, William. 2023. "China's 'Mad Men' Idea For Women To Have Babies To Save Economy." *Forbes*, November 16. https://www.forbes.com/sites/williampesek/2023/11/16/chinas-mad-men-idea-for-women-to-have-babies-to-save-economy/

Peterson, Lisa and O'Hare, Denis. 2014. *An Iliad.* Penguin.

Phelan, John Leddy. 1968. "Pan-Latinism, French Intervention in Mexico (1861-1867) and the Genesis of the Idea of Latin America." In *Conciencia y autenticidad históricas Escritos en homenaje a Edmundo O' Gorman* edited by Juan Antonio Ortega y Medina. UNAM.

Plokhy, Serhii. 2015. *The Gates of Europe. A History of Ukraine.* Basic Books.

Plokhy, Serhii. 2024. "Дякую, Україно! Російсько-українська війна: історична перспектива." In *Війна і нові горизонти* edited by Dmytro Kuleba. Knygolove.

Posner, Eric. 2025. "What Happened to International Law?" *Project Syndicate,* January 16. https://www.project-syndicate.org/commentary/international-law-becoming-irrelevant-amid-backlash-to-globalization-by-eric-posner-2025-01

Quinn, Josephine. 2024. *How the World Made the West. A 4,000 Year History.* Random House.

Regan, Mitt and Sari, Aurel. 2024. *Hybrid Threats and Grey Zone Conflict.* Oxford University Press.

Reuters. 2023. "Russian President Putin Makes Keynote Speech." Reuters, October 5. https://www.reuters.com/world/europe/russian-president-putin-makes-keynote-speech-sochi-2023-10-05/

Rice, Condoleezza. 2024. "The Perils of Isolationism. The World Still Needs America – And America Still Needs the World." Foreign Affairs, August 20. https://www.foreignaffairs.com/united-states/perils-isolationism-condoleezza-rice

Risen, Clay. 2025. *Red Scare.* Scribner.

Rivkin, D. and Casey, L. 2001. "The Rocky Shoals of International Law." *The National Interest* 62: 35–45.

Roberts, Anthea. 2017. *Is International Law International?* Oxford University Press.

Roca, María Elvira. 2020. *Imperiofobia y leyenda negra. Roma, Rusia, Estados Unidos y el Imperio español*, 27th ed. Siruela.

Rodogno, Davide. 2011. "The 'principles of humanity' and the European powers' intervention Ottoman Lebanon and Syria in 1860-1861." In *Humanitarian Intervention: A History,* edited by Brendan Simms and D.J.B. Trim. Cambridge University Press.

Rodriguez, Philippe-André. 2015. "Human dignity as an essentially contested concept." *Cambridge Review of International Affairs* 28 (4): 743–756.

Roth, Philip. 1998. *American Pastoral.* Vintage.

Roth, Philip. 2005. *The Plot Against America*. Vintage.

Rousseau, Jean-Jacques. 2022. *The Social Contract and the First and Second Discourses* Yale University Press.

Rousseau, Martine and Houdart, Olivier. 2007. "There's a Word for People Like You." *The New York Times*, July 6. https://www.nytimes.com/2007/07/06/opinion/06rousseau.html

RSI. 2022. "Russian Military Doctrine Primer." *RSI,* n/d. https://oe.tradoc.army.mil/wp-content/uploads/2022/06/RSI-Russian-Military-Doctrine-Primer-Final-single-page-04282022.pdf

Ryan, Mick. 2023. *White Sun War. The Campaign for Taiwan.* Casemate.

Said, Edward. 1994. *Orientalism*. Vintage.

Sands, Philippe. 2016. *East West Street*. Weidenfeld & Nicolson.

Sands, Philippe. 2021. *The Ratline*. Weidenfeld & Nicolson.

Sands, Philippe. 2022. *The Last Colony.* Weidenfeld & Nicolson.

Sands, Philippe. 2025. *Londres 38: On Impunity, Pinochet in London and a Nazi in Patagonia*. Weidenfeld & Nicolson.

Sanghera, Sathnam. 2021. *Empireland: How Imperialism Has Shaped Modern Britain.* Viking.

Sanghera, Sathnam. 2024. *Empireworld: How British Imperialism Has Shaped the Globe.* Viking.

Schmitt, Carl. 2007. *The Concept of the Political.* The University of Chicago Press.

Seinfeld, Jerry. 2008. "Jerry Seinfeld on Immigration." Truth Be Told, October 5. https://www.youtube.com/watch?v=8l_u5fvB15Q

Shinohara, Hatsue. 2006. "Drift towards an Empire? The Trajectory of American Reformers in the Cold War." In *International Law and Empire: Historical Explorations,* edited by Martti Koskenniemi. Oxford University Press.

Shohat, Ella. 1992. "Notes on the "Post-Colonial." *Social Text* 31/32: 99–113.

Shore, Marci, Snyder, Timothy, and Stanley, Jason. 2025. "We're Experts in Fascism. We're Leaving the U.S." *The New York Times*, May 18. https://www.nytimes.com/2025/05/14/opinion/yale-canada-fascism.html

Sloterdijk, Peter. 2010. *Rage and Time.* Columbia University Press.

Smith, Stacey. 2023. "She had a dream job. Now, she's part of a massive brain drain hammering Russia." *NPR*, May 31. https://www.npr.org/2023/05/31/1176769042/russia-economy-brain-drain-oil-prices-flee-ukraine-invasion

Snyder, Timothy. 2015. *Bloodlands. Europe between Hitler and Stalin.* Vintage.

Snyder, Timothy. 2024. "Ukrainian History and the Future of the World". *LMC,* May 16. https://lmc.icds.ee/lennart-meri-lecture-2024-ukrainian-history-and-the-future-of-the-world-by-timothy-snyder/

Snyder, Timothy. 2024. "Історія України та світу." In *Війна і нові горизонти* edited by Dmytro Kuleba. Knygolove.

SOAS. 2018. "Learning and Teaching Toolkit for Programme and Module Convenors." *SOAS,* n/d. https://blogs.soas.ac.uk/decolonisingsoas/learning-teaching/toolkit-for-programme-and-module-convenors/

Sora, Mihai et al. 2024. "The Great Game in the Pacific Islands." *Lowy Institute*, August. https://interactives.lowyinstitute.org/features/great-game-in-the-pacific-islands/

Spektor, Matias. 2023. "In Defense of the Fence Sitters. What the West Gets Wrong About Hedging." Foreign Affairs, April 18. https://www.foreignaffairs.com/world/global-south-defense-fence-sitters.

Spektor, Matias. 2024. "The US, the West, and international law in an age of strategic competition." Brookings, April 15. https://www.brookings.edu/articles/the-us-the-west-and-international-law-in-an-age-of-strategic-competition/

Srinivasan, Amia. 2022. *The right to sex.* Bloomsbury.

Stavans, Ilan. 2022. "The Dark History of Colonia Dignidad." *The Nation*, March 22. https://www.thenation.com/article/culture/sinister-sect-colonia-dignidad

Steinbeck, John. 1952. *East of Eden.* Viking Press.

Stent, Angela. 2023. *Putin's World. Russia Against the West and With the Rest.* Twelve.

Stouffer. 2023. "Did Shakespeare Really Mean It When He Said, 'Let's Kill All the Lawyers'?" *Stouffer*, July 17. https://www.stoufferlegal.com/blog/did-shakespeare-really-mean-it-when-he-said-lets-kill-all-the-lawyers

Sudyn, Danylo. 2022. "Orcs and Men: How Tolkien helps us understand what's wrong with Russia and its people." *Tyzhden,* April 13. https://tyzhden.ua/orcs-and-men-how-tolkien-helps-us-understand-what-s-wrong-with-russia-and-its-people

Supreme Court of Canada. 1998. "Reference re Secession of Quebec." *SCC*, August 20. https://decisions.scc-csc.ca/scc-csc/scc-csc/en/item/1643/index.do

Supreme Court of the United States. 1967. Afroyim v. Rusk. 387 U.S. 253, 87 S.Ct. 1660, 18 L.Ed.2d 757.

Susman, Dan et al. 2016. "Patrick Stewart sketch: what has the ECHR ever done for us?" *The Guardian*, April 25. https://www.theguardian.com/culture/video/2016/apr/25/patrick-stewart-sketch-what-has-the-echr-ever-done-for-us-video

Tamanaha, Brian. 2004. *On the Rule of Law: History, Politics, Theory*. Cambridge University Press.

Tharoor, Ishan. 2024a. "The war in Gaza looms over Asia's geopolitics." *The Washington Post*, June 5. https://www.washingtonpost.com/world/2024/06/05/asia-gaza-support-israel-china-sympathies-geopolitics-war/

Tharoor, Ishan. 2024b. "What Taiwan is learning from the war in Ukraine." *The Washington Post*, July 1. https://www.washingtonpost.com/world/2024/07/01/taiwan-lessons-ukraine-war-china/

Tharoor, Ishan. 2024c. "Zelensky comes to Asia and scolds China." *The Washington Post*, June 3. https://www.washingtonpost.com/world/2024/06/03/ukraine-asia-china-russia-security-support-shangrila-dialogue/

Tharoor, Ishan. 2025. "In Asia, Hegseth warns against China, but few want to pick sides." *The Washington Post*, June 1. https://www.washingtonpost.com/world/2025/06/01/asia-hegseth-china-shangrila-dialogue-security-summit-sides-trade/

The Bulwark. 2025. "MAGA Is BIGGER THAN TRUMP And There's NO GOING BACK (w/ Annie Karni)." *The Bulwark*, March 26. https://www.youtube.com/watch?v=JdjnnU0y914

The Daily Show. 2025. "Jon Stewart on how Democrats' 'Trump fever' obsession is distracting them from success." *The Daily Show*, March 21. https://www.youtube.com/watch?v=UBvoG7pBc1A

The Post Millennial. 2025. "Sen. John Kennedy." *The Post Millennial*, April 29. https://x.com/TPostMillennial/status/1917249811020984771

The Wall Street Journal. 2025. "These New Chinese Ships Could Bring a D-Day-Style Invasion to Taiwan." *The Wall Street Journal*, May 14. https://www.youtube.com/watch?v=DtrGMsGsZiU

The White House. 2023. "FACT SHEET: President Biden Issues Executive Order on Safe, Secure, and Trustworthy Artificial Intelligence." *The White House*, October 30. https://www.whitehouse.gov/briefing-room/statements-releases/2023/10/30/fact-sheet-president-biden-issues-executive-order-on-safe-secure-and-trustworthy-artificial-intelligence/

Thiong'o, Ngũgĩ wa. 2005. *Decolonising the Mind. The Politics of Language in African Literature*. East African Educational Publishers.

Thucydides. 1989. *The Peloponnesian War. The Complete Hobbes Translation*. The University of Chicago Press.

Torigian, Joseph. 2024. "Xi Jinping's Russian Lessons." *Foreign Affairs,* June 24. https://www.foreignaffairs.com/print/node/1131873

Torres, Ritchie. 2025. "The Rising Democratic Coalition Fell. Now What?" *FP*, January 19. https://www.thefp.com/p/ritchie-torres-the-rising-democratic-coalition-fell-trump-inauguration

Totten, Michael J. 2012. *Where the West Ends.* Belmont Estate Books.

Tripathi, Sali. 2004. "Gandhi, for one, would have found it funny." *The New York Times*, January 21. https://www.nytimes.com/2004/01/21/opinion/meanwhile-gandhi-for-one-would-have-found-it-funny.html

Trujillo, Joaquín. 2019. *Andrés Bello. Libertad, Imperio, Estilo*. Roneo.

UK Government. 2023. "The Bletchley Declaration by Countries Attending the AI Safety Summit, 1-2 November 2023." *UK Government*, November 2. https://www.gov.uk/government/publications/ai-safety-summit-2023-the-bletchley-declaration/the-bletchley-declaration-by-countries-attending-the-ai-safety-summit-1-2-november-2023

Ukraine World. 2024. "Timothy Snyder in Kharkiv: A Conversation about Freedom - with Volodymyr Yermolenko." Ukraine World, December 4. https://ukraineworld.org/en/podcasts/ep-340

UN Human Rights Council. 2008. *Report of the Working Group on the Universal Periodic Review of the United Kingdom of Great Britain and Northern Ireland, A/HRC/8/25*. United Nations.

UNESCO. 1945. "UNESCO Constitution." *UNESCO*, n/d. https://www.unesco.org/en/legal-affairs/constitution

US Senate. 2014. "Report of the Senate Select Committee on Intelligence." US Senate, December 9. https://www.intelligence.senate.gov/sites/default/files/publications/CRPT-113srpt288.pdf

Vargas Llosa, Mario. 2010. *El Sueño del Celta.* Alfaguara.

Varoufakis, Yanis. 2024. *Technofeudalism: What Killed Capitalism.* Melville.

Vázquez Benítez, Rodrigo. 2020. "Legal Operations: The Use of Law as an Instrument of Power in the Context of Hybrid Threats and Strategic Competition." *NATO Legal Gazette* 41: 138–144.

Waldron, Jeremy. 2021. "The Rule of Law as an Essentially Contested Concept." In *The Cambridge Companion to the Rule of Law* edited by Jens Meierhenrich and Martin Loughlin. Cambridge University Press.

Watkins, Devin. 2025. "Pope Leo XIV: News media should foster peace and disarm words." Vatican News, May 12. https://www.vaticannews.va/en/pope/news/2025-05/pope-leo-xiv-media-professionals-audience-conclave.html

Weber, Colonel Jeremy S. 2019. "Playing the MIDFIELD. It's High Time to Recognize Law as an Instrument of National Power." *JAG Reporter,* November 4. https://www.jagreporter.af.mil/Post/Article-View-Post/Article/2548732/playing-the-midfield/

Weintraub, S. and Jones, 'T. "'Civil War' Stars Discuss Filming the 'What Kind of American Are You' Scene." *Collider,* April 13. https://collider.com/civil-war-kirsten-dunst-cailee-spaeny/

Williams, Zoe. 2025. "It's been a big, beautiful week of bad news for Trump. But don't expect it to stick." *The Guardian*, May 29. https://www.theguardian.com/commentisfree/2025/may/29/donald-trump-elon-musk-doge-tariffs

Wortzel, Larry M. 2014. *The Chinese People's Liberation Army and Information Warfare* Strategic Studies Institute, U.S. Army War College.

Xiaolin, D. and Yitong, L. 2022. "The Rise and Fall of China's Wolf Warrior Diplomacy." *The Diplomat,* September 22. https://thediplomat.com/2023/09/the-rise-and-fall-of-chinas-wolf-warrior-diplomacy/

Yglesias, Matthew. 2020. *One Billion Americans. The Case for Thinking Bigger.* Penguin.

Zakaria, Fareed. 2024. *Age of Revolutions. Progress and Backlash from 1600 to the Present.* W.W. Norton and Company.

Note on Indexing

Our books do not have indexes due to the prohibitive cost of assembling them. If you are reading this book in paperback and want to find a particular word or phrase you can do so by downloading a free PDF version of this book from the E-International Relations website. View the e-book in any standard PDF reader and enter your search terms in the search box. You can then navigate through the search results and find what you are looking for. If you are using apps (or devices) to read our e-books, you should also find word search functionality in those.

You can find all of our books at http://www.e-ir.info/publications

www.ingramcontent.com/pod-product-compliance
Lightning Source LLC
Chambersburg PA
CBHW051737020426
42333CB00014B/1357